© BILL MATTOS 2013

All rights reserved. No part of this publication
may be reproduced or stored in a retrieval system
or transmitted, in any form or by any means,
electronic, mechanical, photocopying, recording
or otherwise, without prior permission in writing
from Haynes Publishing.

First published in April 2013

Bill Mattos has asserted his moral right
to be identified as the author of this work.

A catalogue record for this book is
available from the British Library

ISBN 978 0 85733 256 1

Library of Congress control no. 2012948690

Published by Haynes Publishing,
Sparkford, Yeovil, Somerset BA22 7JJ, UK
Tel: 01963 442030 Fax: 01963 440001
Int. tel: +44 1963 442030 Int. fax: +44 1963 440001
E-mail: sales@haynes.co.uk
Website: www.haynes.co.uk

Haynes North America Inc.
861 Lawrence Drive, Newbury Park,
California 91320, USA

While every effort is taken to ensure the accuracy
of the information given in this book, no liability can
be accepted by the author or publishers for any loss,
damage or injury caused by errors in, or omissions
from the information given.

Printed in the USA by Odcombe Press LP,
1299 Bridgestone Parkway, La Vergne, TN 37086

THE ESSENTIAL GUIDE TO ALL KINDS OF KAYAKING

BILL MATTOS

SEA KAYAKING ■ SIT-ON KAYAKS ■ WHITE WATER ■ KAYAK FISHING ■ COMPETITION

CONTENTS

INTRODUCTION

Welcome to the Haynes *Kayaking Manual*. In preparing this manual, I've tried to cover all the important techniques and equipment needed for kayaking, in a way that's both approachable and comprehensible for beginners but equally interesting and inspirational to the accomplished paddler. Even someone who has nothing to learn from such a book may find the photos, anecdotes and quotations thought-provoking or amusing. Or that's my intention anyway...

Because of this, I haven't necessarily explained every technical term in endless detail, but have instead included a glossary at the end. So if you come across a word or expression you haven't heard before (if only because I've made it up!), then with a little luck you'll be able to look it up before you carry on.

Having said that I've aimed to make this book eminently suitable for beginners, I also feel that there's little point expending a lot of words on things that you'll work out for yourself after one minute sitting in a kayak. Instead I've attempted to cover more of the subtle stuff that's rarely included in books of this nature – stuff that will make a real difference to the quality of your experience. Maybe...

I'm very grateful that many of the best and most interesting kayakers in the world today have been kind enough to contribute their thoughts and photographs to the book. Kayaking is a sport that has an almost tribal sense of belonging, and paddlers of all backgrounds and interests treat fellow boaters almost as family, and are always willing to offer help and advice. So I welcome you to this kayaking family, and look forward to meeting you on the water sometime.

Bill Mattos
March 2013

Most kayaking books begin with something like 'Kayaking has been a fundamental blah blah blah since yada yada yada,' etc, so I'm not going to do that. I'm going to begin by telling you exactly what kayaking isn't, so that there's no confusion. Because this manual is about kayaking, and I wouldn't want you to be mixing it up with anything else. Rowing, for instance, or canoeing.

Rowing boats are propelled with oars, which are loosely attached to and pivoted on the boat. The person or persons doing the rowing almost always face backwards, because they can row more powerfully that way.

But canoes and kayaks are propelled by paddles. Paddles are different from oars, mainly in that they aren't attached to the boat at all, but just held in the hands, and unlike rowers the paddlers generally (OK, always) face forwards.

Canoes are paddled with a single-bladed paddle whereas kayaks are paddled with a double-bladed paddle.

Another point worth making is that kayakers typically sit with their legs extended in front of them, whereas in other types of boat there's a wide variety of seating, kneeling or standing positions that might be adopted.

Why all this nomenclature? Well...

The word kayak is quite specific. It comes directly from the Inuit language, also called Inuktitut. Kayak, or *qajaq* as it is usually spelt by the Greenland Inuit today, means 'man's boat' or 'hunter's boat'. There's no ambiguity in that – aboriginally, all men were hunters in their culture. Broadly similar boats were evolved by all of the Arctic races, including the Inuit (across what we now call Canada and between Baffin and Scandinavia), Aleutians (Russia and Alaska) and Ainu (Russia and Japan). Knowing as we do now the fearsome prowess of these kayak paddlers, it's unlikely that there was no interaction between these cultures, which may be why their boats vary only slightly. All designed and built their kayaks using their own experience and that of the previous generation. The knowledge was passed on through oral tradition, since they didn't use writing as we know it.

A kayak was always long, narrow, enclosed and propelled by a two-bladed paddle. That's what worked for an offshore hunting craft. The Inuit did also have bigger boats, called *umniak*, that were often open-cockpit and propelled by single-bladed paddles, and would now be called canoes. They bore a strong resemblance to native American open canoes, unsurprisingly. But a kayak is a kayak.

⬆ **This is a rowing scull. Looks a bit like a kayak. Isn't.**

⬇ **This is an open canoe. Single-bladed paddle. Canoe.**

⬆ **This is a modern sea kayak, inspired by traditional Inuit boats.**

⬇ **Inuit seal hunter with harpoon, paddling slide-hand Greenland-style.**

CABALLITOS DE TOTORA

The people of the mid-coastal region of Peru have used totora reeds to build a type of narrow fishing boat called a *caballito*. These *caballitos de totora*, small rowed or paddled boats, have existed for at least 3,000 years, as evidenced by dating fragments of pottery in the area. It's still common to find clay pots representing these traditional fishing vessels, and the boats themselves are still made by fishermen to this day. While they're not consistently paddled kayak-fashion, the archaeological evidence is that the double-bladed paddle appears to have at least been one of the options as far back as we can currently date them, so I've included these boats for the sake of completeness. And because they're pretty.

→ *Caballito* in the sunset, Peru.
(*Steve Childs*)

CHAPTER 1

FOR STARTERS

When taking up kayaking it behoves us to choose a suitable kayak and paddle, to dress appropriately for the conditions, and to store, transport and use the kayak safely, while still having a really good time!

TAKING UP KAYAKING

It's nice to go paddling. If you have a soul, you probably derive some joy from being on the water, even if you just float about gently, trailing your hands in the water in wonderment. At the other extreme, some people like to hurtle down terrifying turbulent rapids, off gigantic waterfalls, or undertake open ocean crossings that would have daunted Christopher Columbus. Perhaps you have some idea where you'd like to end up. Perhaps none at all. But we all have to start somewhere.

No matter what kind of paddling you're inspired by, it's pretty important to have the basic skills and fitness to get your boat to the water. And then you're going to want to make it go along, stop and turn. So that's what I'm going to cover first. If you already have that stuff down, then go ahead and skip forward through the book until you find something that's interesting for you.

You may gather that I don't like to take life too seriously, and that I'm not a stickler for rules and regulations. But I still firmly believe that if you can't swim, you shouldn't be anywhere near water. It just doesn't make any sense. Water competence is something you can only learn

from a bit of practise and experience, and even if the water is shallow enough to stand in, you can get yourself in a right old mess if you aren't a swimmer. So, if swimming isn't part of your skill set today, don't even think about going kayaking until you've sorted that out. I would say that being able to swim 50m unaided in normal clothing including shoes is a safe minimum for venturing afloat in any kind of boat. You never know when you might end up in the water.

Now that you can swim, let's turn our attention to basic fitness. Now, I'm sure some people are going to say you should have a full medical before going kayaking, but let's be sensible. Basic kayaking isn't strenuous. What's strenuous is lifting your boat on and off the car, swimming, and climbing on to the kayak in the water, that sort of thing. I find it pretty exhausting anyway. So, if you've passed the basic swimming criterion above, and you've managed to carry your boat to the river or tie it on the car unaided, I think you're going to be OK. Clearly, if you have some sort of pre-existing medical condition then you should consider the implications of that, or ask for professional advice. A medical professional, that is. I'm no use to you on that account.

⬇ **All kayakers should make sure they can swim 50m, and not just in a heated pool. It's good to do this under the supervision of someone who can help if it turns out that you can't!**

WHAT TYPE OF BOAT?

ere's where people of different persuasions start to part company. The easiest type of boat to learn all kinds of different stuff in, in order to become a fully rounded kayaker, is a thing we often call a 'general purpose' or GP boat. This is usually a closed-cockpit kayak (meaning that your legs are inside), short enough to manoeuvre easily, and long enough to be fast enough go on little journeys, so very much a jack of all trades and a master of none. Good for learning in, though, and an ideal launch pad from which to learn how to be a competition paddler, a whitewater boater or a sea or surf kayaker. Or any specific discipline really.

If you don't want to learn all kinds of stuff and become a fully rounded kayaker – for instance because you just want to paddle a stable touring or family-fun boat – you may want to skip the GP boat phase and go straight to the sit-on or large cockpit boat that you're going to use. You can learn all the skills that are relevant to your ambitions right there in the boat you ultimately want to own.

⬆ **A sit-on-top kayak is a good choice for most beginners on calm water.**

⬅ **The general-purpose closed-cockpit kayak is perfect for learning almost all kayaking skills.**

If you want to be a surf kayaker, I suggest you start with a sit-on-top kayak, then take it out in small waves when you're ready to, provided there's no one around to crash into. Then learn to roll really well in a borrowed GP boat, and then buy a surf kayak!

If you only want to paddle on flat water, for instance in race boats, then join a club or group that will help you learn the basics in GP boats, and progress immediately to fast touring or skinny race kayaks.

As for sea kayakers, some people do start out and stay in a sea kayak from the outset. But I'd suggest that there are a lot of strokes and skills that are much easier to learn in a GP boat, or even a sit-on kayak.

I should also mention the options of inflatable and folding kayaks. These are wonderfully practical things, because you can deflate them

⬆⬆ **This is a specialist surf kayak complete with fins. You'd be kinda crazy to try to learn to paddle or roll in one, and irresponsible to take it in the surf until you can.**

⬆ **Fast touring or racing kayaks are far too unstable for your first attempts at kayaking.**

➡ **A plastic sea or touring kayak is stable, easy to paddle and roll, and practical. But you might find basic strokes are harder to learn in one.**

or fold them up and put them in the back of the car, and store them much more easily at home. I think it's fair to say that their performance is often slightly compromised compared to a rigid boat of a similar nature, but maybe not so much as to outweigh the advantages. What is complicated, though, is that they come in many forms. There are inflatable boats that very much resemble a sit-on-top kayak, or share the same advantages anyway, of unsinkability and 'easy to climb back on'-ness. There are both inflatable and folding kayaks that are more analogous to the open-cockpit touring kayak, and some which are very close to being full-on sea kayaks. So, keep these options in mind when you realise that the only place you can keep your boat is the cupboard under the stairs!

A word of warning about older fibreglass kayaks. If you have a really tight budget (or have just found a kayak skulking in the garden) you may end up having a go in an older slalom kayak, or something derived from one anyway. Up until the 1980s pretty much all general-purpose kayaks were either older slalom designs, or developed pretty much directly from them. This means fibreglass, 4m (13ft) long, and 60cm (2ft) wide, with a very small cockpit, a hard fibreglass bucket seat, and usually lots of sharp edges inside and out. I'm not knocking this – many of the best kayakers around today learnt to paddle in boats like these. But please be aware that they're difficult to get into and, more importantly, out of, very hard to paddle in a straight line, and likely to give you a backache unless you're quite an athlete. So if you can get your hands on something plastic, and safer, I'd recommend it. Unless you want to be a slalom racer.

⬇ **A folding kayak with room for two.**

⬆ **A typical inflatable kayak.**

⬇ **Slalom boats can be really cheap, or free. The top one is a fairly modern slalom kayak, which is a pretty extreme thing to be paddling at the best of times. Even on calm water, if you stop paddling it'll veer one way or the other, and then you'll probably trip over one of the edges. The lower one is an old GP boat derived from a slalom design – a bit roomier, but still not the safest choice for a beginner.**

KNOW YOUR KAYAKS

2 SIMPLE TOURING BOAT

Stable, easy to paddle medium distances and to keep in a straight line. This one has a fairly small cockpit but they can have larger openings making them very unscary for beginners.

1 SIT ON TOP

A stable, unsinkable boat that's suitable for beginners, but also very good for gentle touring, and excellent for fishing.

3 CREEK BOAT

Designed for running whitewater rivers. Basic versions without all the hardcore features are also used as general purpose kayaks for learning in.

4 **PLAYBOAT**

Specifically for doing tricks on white water, and not a great deal of use for anything else, but they are very stable on flat water and can be used to give a beginner confidence.

5 **SEA KAYAK**

Based on traditional Inuit designs, these kayaks are perfect for long distances in wind, swells or choppy water. But they are relatively unstable, and tend to have smallish cockpit openings.

6 **RACING KAYAK**

Also known as a training/fitness kayak. Fast in a straight line, not very easy to manoeuvre, and desperately unstable. The large cockpit makes it easy to get in and out though.

7 **SLALOM KAYAK**

A very extreme design suited only for slalom racing/training in controlled conditions. Usually very light and fragile.

8 **SQUIRT BOAT**

A crazy low volume kayak used for sub-/ trans-surface tricks on flat water or in rapids. Very difficult to get in and out of the cockpit. Rolling skills essential. Dangerous for anyone not already expert on white water.

9 **SURF KAYAK**

A very directional boat with a surfboard-like hull, suitable for surfing in the ocean by experts only.

Plastic or composite? Plastic kayaks are pretty heavy and tiring to carry. Composite kayaks are pretty fragile, and you won't want to put them down on a hard surface. There isn't really much middle ground, though at the time of writing various technologies like thermoforming are proposing a viable compromise. But for most people, it's one or the other.

Plastic boats are rotomoulded from polyethylene. It's like immensely strong Tupperware. They're very droppable and draggable, and weather a lot of abuse and incompetence.

Boats made from composite materials like fibreglass, carbon fibre or mixtures, like this epoxy-carbon-Kevlar example, can be super-strong, but usually they're made to be super-light. They're easily scratched, cracked or dinged, but composites are the material of choice for most high-performance boats.

PLASTIC

COMPOSITE

HANDLES
Moulded-in handles are a feature of many plastic kayaks, and make it simple and convenient to carry them, or tie them to things.

FOOTREST

HATCH

DECK LINES
Many larger kayaks feature deck lines (ropes) that make it easier to manhandle the boat, and to hang on to it after a swim. These are often supplemented with shockcord or cargo netting for storage of bits and bobs you might need to hand.

HOLES
Sit-on-top kayaks have holes in them. Yes, holes. This is because the shape is basically a tub, and if it didn't have drain holes it would fill up. This means there's no way to keep dry, because as soon as you start paddling water splashes up through the holes.

DRAIN PLUG

SEAT

BACKREST

COCKPIT
Closed cockpit kayaks are not really 'closed' but they have a small opening so that the knees and feet are under the deck.

| TIP | BACK FACE | THROAT | SHAFT | OVAL | DRIVE FACE |

HULL SHAPES

Entry-level sit-on kayaks often have complex hull shapes in an attempt to combine some performance with confidence and stability. Like everything, they're a compromise.

Some boats have rounded hulls, and some have 'chines' or corners. Chines give a more positive feel for better dynamic control, but a more twitchy feel in turbulent or reactive conditions.

If a boat is wider in front of the cockpit, it's called fish-shaped. If wider behind, it's called 'Sweden-form'. Boat designers use the plan shape to determine where the centre of lift is in relation to the centre of pressure, to optimise certain performance characteristics. Phew! It's also nice, if the boat needs to be wider, if the wide bit is out of the way of where you're trying to stick the paddle in!

← **A sit-on kayak hull.**

→ **A rounded kayak hull.**

→ → **Chines visible on a semi-displacement kayak hull.**

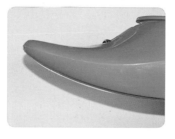

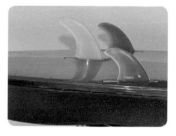

SEA ENDS

The ends of a sea kayak are upturned to cut through waves and provide control in crosswinds.

CREEK ENDS

River-running boats have rounded ends to help them surface quickly in rapids, and for bouncing off rocks and avoiding entrapments.

PLAY ENDS

Playboats have very low, flat ends that can slice easily into the water to facilitate tricks and three-dimensional paddling.

SURF FINS

Surf kayaks have fins like a surfboard, and flat hulls with hard rails. Like a surfboard. Go figure...

BASIC EQUIPMENT

In order to kayak responsibly, you will need three things: a kayak, a paddle, and a buoyancy aid or PFD. If you're not kayaking in isolation, or in a naturist colony, it may also be socially advantageous to wear some sort of clothing, and what you choose to wear will depend very much on the circumstances and the climate. So we'll leave that until later.

BUOYANCY AIDS

First of all, some definitions. A 'buoyancy aid' is any piece of equipment worn or held which is intended to help keep you afloat, and is suitable for use by swimmers when rescue is close at hand. In the EC, it's illegal to sell anything as a 'buoyancy aid' unless it conforms to at least one of a range of CE standards. This will be indicated by a 'CE' logo inside, and a bunch of other numbers that mean very little to the user but indicate exactly which standard it meets.

← No buoyancy aid, on fast-flowing murky water, far from shore and with steep muddy banks and difficult egress, doesn't get my vote of confidence.

⬇ No buoyancy aid in warm, clear, shallow water close to the shore and help is understandable, and stops you from getting a funny sun-tan.

⬇ **A typical CE-approved buoyancy aid or personal flotation device, with a zipped front opening, adjustable retaining or 'compression' straps, and a pocket. This one is a good choice since it's suitable for any sort of kayaking (until you get to really extreme) and cut short enough to use in most types of boat.**

Incidentally, 'PFD' – or personal flotation device – is the American name for a buoyancy aid, with a different legal standard administered by the US Coastguard. You can pretty much assume that any device bearing either the USCG or the CE standard is a fairly reliable one, but the standard only covers the basics and means it fits most normal people, doesn't float them the wrong way up, and has passed some (minor) strength and durability tests.

The buoyancy aid is something that some people regard as optional. It isn't. Really. Most people, most of the time, will be safer wearing a buoyancy aid, and even if you're one of the few who falls outside that category, it'll be setting a better example to those who do need one if you conform and take one as well. Obviously, be careful you don't get a dodgy tan. Priorities.

However, you will see people paddling without a buoyancy aid/PFD, and in particular you may notice that people on stand-up paddle-boards (SUPs), and surfers in particular, almost never wear them. So what's that all about? Are kayakers simply doomed to look uncool?

Having said that it's always safer to wear a PFD than not, let me qualify that with some more info so that we can tell who's not wearing one out of informed choice, and who's taking an unnecessary risk. Most people – those who've graduated past the water wings phase anyway – don't wear any kind of flotation device to go swimming, even in the sea.

No buoyancy aid in warm, clear, shallow water, close to the shore and help, is understandable, and stops you from getting a funny sun-tan. But no buoyancy aid on fast-flowing murky water, far from the shore and with steep muddy banks and difficult egress, doesn't get my vote of confidence.

Surfers and stand-up paddlers don't tend to wear buoyancy aids because they're attached by a leash to a board which is unsinkable and easy to get back on to. A PFD would be redundant, and might even make it more difficult to get back 'on-board'. And in cold, tiring conditions they usually wear a wetsuit, which provides a similar degree of flotation to a PFD.

What about people paddling sit-on kayaks in their swimwear in the sunshine? If you're somewhere that you'd happily swim for fun, with no wind, waves or adverse conditions, the fact that you're using a sit-on-top kayak just makes it all the safer, because you have a big, unsinkable floaty thing to hang on to if you get tired. You don't need to wear a buoyancy aid. If you're paddling another type of kayak that could fill up with water it's a different matter, because managing that in the water, if you were to fall in, is tiring and difficult, so you'd benefit a lot from the extra help a PFD provides. If windy conditions dictate that your boat might blow away from you, a PFD – or at least a wetsuit – will help you stay afloat. A full steamer wetsuit provides almost as much buoyancy as a PFD anyway.

People paddling race K1s never seem to wear PFDs. This is because they paddle, by definition, on very calm inland waters with rescue close at hand. Often they train and race with an actual powered rescue boat shadowing them, or trained lifeguards on the bank. Oh, and they're proper athletes. That's why they don't wear PFDs. However, I'd recommend that anyone going race-boat training without boat or bank support should wear a PFD, because unstable K1 to K1 rescues are super-difficult, and you can get very cold and weary trying to sort out the carnage of a swim.

Kayak surfers often don't wear a PFD. The reasons for this are interesting. First, they paddle amongst surfers, who often regard kayaks with suspicion. Therefore it's often better not to wear a helmet and PFD, because looking as if you're wearing body-armour isn't a good way to ingratiate oneself with the rest of the crowd. Second, you have no business paddling a kayak in the surf around anyone else if there's the slightest possibility that you're going to fall out of it. That may sound harsh, but it's the reality. A waterlogged kayak in the surf is a lethal projectile. Learn to paddle it somewhere else.

Hardcore, usually Canadian, whitewater boaters sometimes paddle without PFDs because they think it looks cool, they like to show off their ripped physiques, and they enjoy the attention and the controversy. But it's incredibly dangerous and, most people feel, a bad influence on less skilful paddlers.

Sea kayakers sometimes paddle without a PFD or carry one under the deck-lines instead of wearing it. Some of these paddlers are making an informed judgement call that they're well within their capabilities. Don't be influenced by that – make your own decision. Could you put a PFD on in the water? Could you manage a swamped sea kayak without a PFD on? Did you actually think you were going to fall in in the first place? No, of course you didn't.

Traditional kayakers also sometimes wear an Inuit-style *tuiliq* (kayaking jacket) made of neoprene wetsuit material. This provides buoyancy comparable to a PFD, which might be why they aren't wearing one of those as well.

There's less argument about the necessity for a kayak and a paddle. The question is, what kind?

The best thing to do is consider the kayak first, because the type of paddle is usually incumbent upon the nature of the boat. The first thing most people think about when selecting a kayak is stability. How

tippy is it going to be? If you're a beginner you want something stable, so that you don't spend all day falling in the water. The downside of stable is that it'll be less manoeuvrable and less responsive to certain advanced techniques, but we aren't there yet are we? It'll probably also be slow, but equally you probably aren't entering a race on day one.

The most accessible type of stable kayak is the sit-on-top boat. This is a completely sealed and unsinkable platform, and you sit on it, not in it, so you don't have to worry about being trapped inside, or not getting a tan on your legs. They're generally really difficult to capsize, on calm water at any rate. However, as I've mentioned, they do nearly always have drain holes in them to let the water out, so it's pretty much impossible to stay completely dry when paddling one.

You may also want to consider a general-purpose boat like the one shown on page 13, or instead learn the basics in a creek boat, a slalom boat or a playboat – they all approximate to the same thing for the complete beginner. Or, as I said in the previous chapter, you could jump straight to the type of boat you want to use. I hope reading these pages and referring to the illustrations will help you to gauge what you might want.

↑ **A good quality entry level paddle with plastic blades and a fibreglass shaft.**

↑ **A premium asymmetric touring paddle made from carbon fibre.**

↑ **A cheerful entry-level or young person's paddle made from tough plastic and with a fibreglass shaft.**

↑ **A lovely wooden touring paddle for the more traditional kayaker.**

↑ **A fibreglass touring paddle with a pronounced rib on the drive face and rubber drip rings.**

↑ **An asymmetric whitewater paddle with a slight rib instead of dihedral.**

→ **An adjustable split-joint that can be set at any angle, and right- or left-handed too.**

PADDLES

When you're paddling a low-performance kayak it doesn't make too much difference if your paddle is very basic. But if you're planning to progress much you'll benefit a lot from the improved feedback a good quality paddle can offer. The better paddle will also probably be lighter and at the same time more durable.

Basic (usually plastic) paddles tend to have quite bendy blades and a rigid metal shaft. This is entirely the wrong way around for skilful or powerful paddling. A good quality paddle will have a fairly stiff blade area, so that the hydrodynamic characteristics of the blade don't vary in the water depending what you're doing with it. The blade should also be light, so that the 'swing weight' of the whole paddle is minimised. This is less tiring for the paddler. The shaft, however, should have enough flex in it to absorb shocks and load, and help reduce the risk of joint, tendon and muscle injury.

The other issue with many cheaper paddles is that they often achieve blade stiffness at the expense of increased thickness/weight, or shapes (like struts) that make the blade less streamlined.

When it comes to blade shapes the options are bewildering, so here's some information to try and help you choose.

Symmetry

Many paddles have an asymmetrical blade shape like most of those shown. This helps the blade go in and out of the water cleanly. The disadvantage is that you have to hold the paddle in the correct orientation. In other words, there's a left and a right, and if you pick it up the wrong way around the blade will be upside down.

Very narrow blades or Greenland-style paddles don't really benefit from asymmetry so it isn't so much of a consideration.

The correct way to hold an asymmetric paddle is shown in the picture above – the shorter side of the blade at the bottom and the long side at the top. It means that the blade makes a clean entry and is balanced in the water, with no twisting forces.

Aspect ratio

An intelligent-sounding expression that means whether the paddle blade is long and thin, or short and fat. A low-ratio blade will have more surface area and less edge length than a high-ratio blade. In undisturbed water both offer similar power characteristics, because, oddly, edge drag is at least as significant as surface area when it comes to power delivery. The long thin blade is also easier to control and move around in the water. However, in aerated (white) water, the short fat blade comes in to its own.

Basically the choices are symmetrical or asymmetrical, long and thin, short and fat, and big feather angle or small.

For this reason, a whitewater paddle or surfing paddle tends to be low aspect ratio, and a sea kayaking or touring paddle may be longer and thinner.

More or less feather

The term 'feather' comes from rowing, not kayaking. It refers to the act of turning the blade after it comes out of the water, to reduce wind resistance. In kayaking, 'feather' also refers to the angle the blades are offset by. It's sometimes called twist, because it's also how much you have to twist the paddle each stroke to put the other blade in the water. On some paddles the feather is adjustable, but usually it's a fixed angle: 90° feather will give you low windage because the blade that isn't in the water when paddling, known as the air blade, is slicing through the air edgeways. The downside is that you have to rotate the paddle a lot between left and right strokes, and that can be exhausting. It also leads to medical problems with your wrists, similar to a repetitive strain injury. So it's rare to find 90° feather these days.

No offset at all, or 0°, is equally rare. It's appealing to beginners because they don't have to learn to feather. However, it just doesn't work very well unless you have a super-skinny Greenland paddle. Most standard paddles fall between 45° and 65°, the lower end for white water and surf, and the higher end for distance paddling. The photo below shows how feathered paddles look. When one blade is horizontal, the other is more upright. This one has about 60° of twist.

Flat, dihedral, scooped or wing

Because the paddler can't exert much rotational leverage gripping a thin paddle shaft, one of the problems is of blades 'fluttering' in the water. This can be improved with one or more ribs down the blade, but then the blade won't slice nicely through the water sideways when you want it to. The solution is called 'dihedral'. This helps the water flow off both sides of the blade to stabilise it. It looks as though it might be inefficient, but because it makes paddling so much easier it's quite the opposite.

The wing blade design evolved in the mid-1980s, taking competitive kayakers in sprint, marathon and downriver away from the scooped asymmetric blade design, the standard in efficient blade design before the invention of the wing.

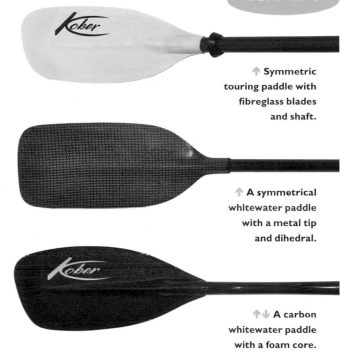

⬆ **Symmetric touring paddle with fibreglass blades and shaft.**

⬆ **A symmetrical whitewater paddle with a metal tip and dihedral.**

⬆⬇ **A carbon whitewater paddle with a foam core.**

⬆ **From the side view you can see that the blade is quite thick. You can also see the cranked shaft in this photo. It's important to grip this in the correct way. (See 'Holding and using the paddle', page 40.)**

⬆ **Traditional Greenland paddle.**

⬆ **A squirt-boat paddle – very small area and very cut away near the neck of the blade.**

PADDLE LENGTH

I stand 6ft (182cm) in height. Here are the typical paddle lengths I generally use for different types of kayaking:

Surfing & freestyle whitewater paddling	185cm (72.8in)
Squirt boating	190cm (74.8in)
Creeking/extreme whitewater	195cm (76.8in)
Flatwater fast touring	200cm (78.7in)
Sea kayaking	215cm (84.6in)

A wing blade creates lift as the blade begins to move tangentially to the boat during the 'pull-through' phase of the stroke. Water then flows over the leading edge, thus creating upforce. The high resistance on the powerside and lift on the backside provides an increased efficiency of around 5%. A well-designed wing will 'find' its own trajectory without flutter, and exits cleanly from the water at the end of the stroke.

Scooped or wing paddles are good for high-speed forward paddling but don't work well for steering and other complex strokes. The standard for whitewater, surf and other manoeuvre-orientated disciplines is the dihedral blade design.

Paddle construction

The number of choices here is bewildering and ever growing. But as well as considering blade stiffness (more is better), one thing to look at is thickness. A thin blade generally feels more incisive and precise in the water, if it's still stiff enough. However, many people like foam-filled blades and wooden blades. These are thicker, but buoyant. Some paddlers consider that the extra buoyancy and support this offers while the blade is in the water is worth the slight increase in thickness. Personally I don't find that an advantage, but so many kayakers do that I think it's best to try both types.

The paddle shaft can be made from any number of materials. The cheapest ones tend to be aircraft-grade aluminium, the more expensive ones from composite materials like fibreglass or carbon. At the time of writing, there's a very popular type of shaft made from epoxy resin and fibreglass that was developed for making pole-vault poles, and it offers an awesome combination of slight flexibility with enormous strength.

Paddle length

The length of paddle you'll require is determined mostly by your height and hence your reach/arm-span. The secondary consideration is what type of paddling you're doing. Many older texts (and instructors) will suggest that the correct length is such that you can just reach over the top of the paddle with your hand when it's standing upright. But nowadays most experts use paddles much shorter than this – the longer paddles used for sea paddling and fast touring are around that length. So, initially and for all-round use I'd suggest a paddle that's around 15cm (6in) taller than your height. However, if you're specialising in a particular type of paddling, you might want to consider some other options.

I have about ten paddles in my bag at the moment, and I use all of them from time to time.

Cranked shafts

The other thing I should mention is the cranked or ergo shaft. When I was a lad and most paddles had an 80–90° feather, it was very common for people to develop wrist problems from kayaking. This was often called tendonitis although I believe the correct medical term for the condition most people experienced is tenosynovitis. Don't quote me though, I'm not a doctor. Anyway, one thing that improved the situation a lot was the introduction of the bent/cranked/ergo shaft, which allowed the paddler to load the wrist at a more natural angle. Which is all good. There are supposed to be some other ergonomic benefits to this grip as well although what they are I have never quite been able to divine. Personally, I never liked them. With a crank you have to grab the paddle in exactly the same place every time, and I like to mix it up a bit more than that. Secondly, the wrist issues that I experienced quite badly went away altogether when I switched down to 45° feather, so I was happy to carry on with a straight shaft. Thirdly, I have never used a crank that felt balanced to me. I don't like to grip the stick too hard, and I think cranks drop to a weird angle instead of sitting in your hand where you left them. Which seems to defeat the object. However I'm very happy to say I could be completely wrong about all of this and maybe you should go and buy one immediately. I'm just not going to... The angle that the arm forms when holding a cranked shaft is much more natural and conducive to good ergonomics and form, as well as reducing stress on the wrist joints.

There are several types of crank, and the names (crank, double crank, modified crank, ergo) applied by different brands cause me some confusion. As I see it they fall into two basic categories: the simpler crank with two bends at each end, which leaves the pulling hand out of alignment with the blade axis, and those with more complex shapes that realign the pull with the blade. The former is torsionally unstable but is preferred by some stronger athletes like slalom paddlers. The latter is more ergonomic but in my opinion still not really balanced if you relinquish your death-grip on the shaft.

SOFT WEAR

What you want to wear while you're kayaking depends mostly on the climate. And perhaps a bit on fashion. And a whole lot upon whether you're actually going to get wet or not. Maybe it's fine to go kayaking in swimwear, but often it's too cold for that, and you might want to wear a wetsuit. Wetsuits vary in severity from the summer shortie or combinations to the full-length steamer wetsuit shown below. Bear in mind that surfing wetsuits have the zip at the back. This is OK, but if the zip is too long it can be uncomfortable in a kayak with a high backrest. For this reason I prefer the combination of neoprene trousers with a neoprene shirt, if wetsuits are the choice on the day.

↑ **A sea kayak paddler wearing a waterproof jacket and a buoyancy aid with pockets.**

A lot of paddlers prefer to wear a windproof shell and as many thermal layers as required by the weather. This can be a lot more comfortable to paddle in, and is OK for a quick dip as long as the water isn't freezing or the air too cold or windy. An even better solution, where immersion is possible rather than probable, is a fibre pile shell of the type often worn by mountaineers. They're a really versatile way of keeping warm, or cool, and they dry out super-quickly if you're moving.

↑ **A thin neoprene shirt and board shorts might be ideal in mild conditions and warm water.**

↑ **A full wetsuit, similar to the ones worn by surfers – rather restricting on the forearms for kayaking.**

↑ **A one-piece drysuit with a back zip is the ultimate in cold conditions. This one is designed especially for kayaking and has a bit to cover the sprayskirt. It can be hard to put on a vest-style buoyancy aid over a drysuit, so choose an opening design.**

↑ **A pair of salopettes, high-waisted trousers, or bib pants. Worn over thermals, these allow you to wade in the water without getting wet, but aren't too hot and bothersome to wear for paddling on fine days.**

SPRAYSKIRT (DECK)

This is the thing that covers the cockpit of the kayak to stop water getting in when you're paddling. It's very possible that you don't need a sprayskirt to begin with, but if you're paddling a closed-cockpit kayak in rough water, or practising more advanced skills that involve leaning the kayak over, you may need one.

If that's the case, you need to be very confident you can pull the sprayskirt off the boat if you need to. It's best to practise this a lot, with your eyes shut. Do make sure that you can find the release handle without needing to see it, and assure yourself you can pull the sprayskirt off easily enough. Otherwise getting out of the boat underwater is no fun at all.

For the four decades I've been paddling, sprayskirts have been one of three basic types. The cheapest are made from waterproofed fabric like canvas, PVC or nylon. At the other extreme we have sprayskirts made from neoprene (wetsuit material) or something very similar. These are better fitting than fabric ones, and very waterproof indeed. In between you may come across neoprene skirts that have a fabric part around the body – these have most of the benefits of the neoprene type but are more comfortable to wear paddling long distances or in hot climates.

← The cheapest kind of sprayskirt is a simple nylon one, but it's pretty unpleasant against your legs and won't protect you in really rough water.

↑ This neoprene deck is robust, nice to use, and has a knee release so you can be confident of kicking it off if you can't reach the handle.

↑ The combination deck is a very comfortable option for long periods of use or in warmer climates.

←↑ Make sure that you can find the release handle without needing to see it, and assure yourself you can pull the sprayskirt off easily enough. Otherwise getting out of the boat underwater is no fun at all.

HELMETS

Helmets for kayaking are, like buoyancy aids, another slightly controversial issue. Many people are introduced to wearing a helmet right from their very first go at paddling, even on flat water. After all, you never know when you're going to bang your head. On the other hand, I've banged my head a lot more on kitchen cupboards than I ever have kayaking, but I rarely don any sort of protective headgear to make a cup of tea. All forms of kayaking competition apart from sprint and marathon require that competitors wear a helmet, but most touring paddlers, sea kayakers and surf kayakers never wear one. That's a personal choice. All whitewater paddlers wear helmets. Not to do so borders on insanity.

There are special safety standards for helmets in Europe and in the US. Kayaking helmets aren't the same specification as similar-looking climbing, skydiving and hockey helmets, so DO make sure that your lid is suitable for kayaking before you use it in the water.

In the past it's often been suggested that a kayaking helmet should have holes in it to let the water out. If it has a cradle inside and sits away from the head, this makes some sense. Some people prefer not to let the water in at all, by having a head-hugging foam lining. This is much warmer and helps the helmet not to get ripped off your head by the current.

A word about peaks on the front of helmets. Many paddlers like them because they act as sun-visors and stop falling water from running into your eyes. I like them because when you're upside down they help to stop rocks from hitting you in the face. But if you're in a situation where you're getting bundled around with other people, like a rescue, or paddling a raft, keep in mind that the peak can injure them.

FOOTWEAR

There are really three choices of footwear for kayaking, assuming that you aren't in a place where bare feet or flip-flops seems to make sense. Normally some sort of protection is required against bashes and scrapes in or on the kayak.

Where space in the boat is an issue, wetsuit socks are good. They aren't good for walking though. Wetsuit boots are better, and watershoes are best but not warm in their own right.

➜ A typical plastic helmet with a chinstrap and adjustable cradle inside.

➜ A more fashionable and expensive composite helmet, but it doesn't necessarily offer more protection and might be ruined after one little bump.

➜ Some whitewater kayakers use full-face helmets or chinguards.

⬆ There are many types of reinforced neoprene socks available. Ordinary ones wear out too easily, but these in the picture above are perfect if boots or shoes won't fit in the kayak.

⬆ Wetsuit boots come in many forms, but I recommend they have thick rubber toes and heels as well as soles.

⬆ I quite often wear an old pair of running shoes with a pair of neoprene socks underneath if required.

⬆ If there's any likelihood of serious climbing/walking/portaging or of swimming in rocky places, consider some proper water shoes.

For many people, their choice to kayak – and their choice of kayak – has already been dictated by where they live, or somewhere they like to go. Perhaps you live near a river, or always go to the seaside on holiday. If you're anything like me, you see someone doing something outdoors, and think to yourself 'That looks cool, I want a piece of that!'

Every piece of water has its challenges. A skilful kayaker can negotiate almost any water, but it takes experience to know what the demands of that particular water are likely to be. Until you have that knowledge, you need to rely on observation and enquiry. Beginners should seek out predictable and sheltered places at first. Big tides, strong currents, wind or waves are to be avoided. But more important than any of these things, and often overlooked, is the matter of access. Is it easy to get afloat (or 'put in', as kayak geeks say), and equally are you going to be able to get out at the other end of your adventure? What if your journey is cut short? Will you be able to get ashore just anywhere, or only in certain places? A lot of people have got into trouble because although they could get to shore, they couldn't get out of the water. So think ahead.

WHERE NOT TO GO PADDLING

There's a short list of scenarios I'm going to mention that a lot of people don't think about. Clearly, you can drown in a puddle if you're stupid, drunk or unlucky enough, but generally we can all look after ourselves. However, most people don't realise the horrendous dangers posed by some common outdoor situations. Here are some obstructions and hazards to watch out for:

Rocks and trees in the current

It's completely counterintuitive to those who don't spend time in moving water, but quite slow currents can be *very* dangerous. If you're walking or swimming and your foot becomes entrapped between rocks, a moderate current can push you over and down, and drowning is a very real danger. Equally, if swimming or paddling a kayak, a gentle current that you could paddle against can pin you so firmly to an obstruction like a bridge, a rock or a fallen tree that you'd not be able to escape. So, until you have some tricks in your hat for these situations, give them a wide berth. And perhaps even when you have.

Weirs

Even experts find it difficult to judge weirs. Sometimes they're harmless and you'll see people playing in them. Sometimes an equally innocuous looking one is quite lethal, either because of the powerful hydraulics and towback, or hidden obstructions under the water. Unless you know a weir to be safe for someone of your ability, don't mess with them. It isn't worth it.

Rips

At the beach there are often unseen currents called rips, especially where there's surf. They can carry you offshore very quickly, whether you're swimming or paddling. This can be quite handy, a free ride so to speak, but if you aren't ready to go to sea it can be a bit dangerous. Make sure you know whether there are rips or other dangerous currents.

⬆ **A current and a fallen tree is a deadly combination. This water is too severe for a beginner too – if you can't be sure you can avoid the obstruction, you really shouldn't be on the river.**

⬆ **Keep a safe distance from weirs. They can be lethal, and often near invisible when approached from above.**

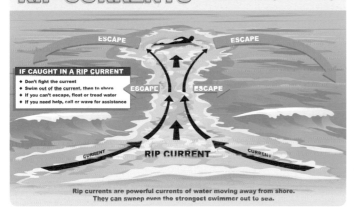

← ↑ **It's not always possible to tell where the rip currents are, but if there's a beach break there's probably a rip.**

Offshore winds

Another reason people get into difficulty at the beach is simply a wind blowing them offshore. You might start out feeling in control, but as you get tired, and maybe the wind gets stronger, you could find yourself struggling to get back. Just think about it, is all I'm saying.

Floods

Some of us spend our kayaking careers chasing floods. But unless you're an expert whitewater boater, don't risk paddling where water levels might suddenly change. Heavy rain, dam releases or just a hot day in a snow-melt region are all reasons why the river level could rise dramatically, increasing in speed, power and complexity and taking you right out of your comfort zone. Places with big tidal variations are also an issue. Not only can there be dangerous waves and currents, but your access to the shore might be compromised if levels change.

Thunderstorms

It's very bad news to be on the water in a boat during a thunderstorm. You're much more likely to be struck by lightning, as the only thing pointing upwards in a wide expanse of flatness – especially if you're holding a big, long carbon-fibre stick in your hands! And although being struck by lightning isn't a barrel of fun wherever it happens, on the water it's infinitely more dangerous. If there's thunder anywhere nearby, get off the water as quickly as possible. And don't shelter under isolated trees.

Sun and dehydration

It's not specific to kayaking, but people do get sunburnt a lot more easily on the water than on land. Think about sunscreen, hats and long-sleeved clothing. It's easy to forget about the sun when you're afloat, and then later you find you're lobster-coloured and sore. The long-term dangers of sun exposure are very real too.

If you don't drink enough water you'll rapidly experience reduced physical and mental function. And there's something about being on the water that makes you forget about drinking until it's too late. Make sure you have a few gulps of water every hour. A lot of people think they need to drink several litres of water a day, but it depends how much you eat as well. Don't forget that most food is 60% water at least. And it's better not to eat and drink at the same time, as this impairs how effectively you can metabolise the food. What I try to do is drink a little one hour, snack a little the next, and repeat.

HEALTH AND SAFETY

One of the things that stops a lot of people from enjoying kayaking safely is the safety-obsessed attitude of those who run clubs and instructional institutions. And don't get me wrong. These people have to be safety Nazis, because if anything goes awry that could have been prevented, they're going to be taking the blame, and will very probably be the target of litigation. This is a bit rubbish, because it makes club leaders and instructors tell everyone that they must wear a helmet and a buoyancy aid and be wrapped up in cotton wool. Even in the shower.

This sort of nonsense has made an adventure sport into an exercise in shopping. Because of course, the retail outfitters aren't going to miss the opportunity to sell you gear. So the nanny state conspires with corporate cynicism to make you go out kayaking dressed like a total numpty.

So, which is more dangerous? Going out kayaking in your everyday clothes with no buoyancy aid, albeit on a sunny day and calm waters; or dressing from head to foot in the latest body armour and safety gear and hurling yourself off a 100ft waterfall?

I don't need to tell you that it's the latter, by quite a significant margin – but proponents of waterfall kayaking are seen as somewhat heroic hooligans, whereas the average Joe having a sedate paddle is regarded as an irresponsible villain. Why?

I think it's important to make informed decisions. Knowledge is the key to that – if you don't know anything, you can't make an informed call. Certainly, putting other people in danger to rescue or evacuate you is irresponsible. But if you're pretty sure you're no more likely to embroil pedestrian observers or the professional rescue services in your adventure than you would be when walking down the street, then where's the harm?

So, read this book, and then think about it some more, and make your own decisions.

Less than three

One of the things I read – and was repeatedly told when I started kayaking – is never to go alone, and ideally go in a group of three people or more. The adage was 'less than three there never should be'. This odd piece of advice stemmed from the idea that if one of the party was injured, someone could stay with the victim while the other went for help. Alone. I never really thought it made sense.

Many adventure sports have their solo practitioners, and the very principle of being alone and having no margin for error is part of the appeal for some. It's not strange or irresponsible to go for a hike alone, or drive a car alone, so I see no reason why kayaking alone should be frowned upon. However, it might be kind to let loved ones know when to expect your return, and to have some way to ameliorate any delays or problems. A cellphone, a VHF radio, or a GPS with emergency comms out feature could save your life, and just as importantly could stop your family from worrying about you every time you go out!

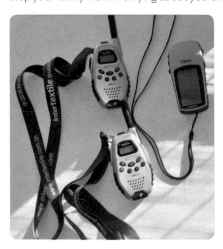

← **VHF radios, or cellphones where coverage exists, allow you to keep in touch and/or call for help, food or a shuttle. A GPS is useful so that you can tell people where you are!**

It's a well-documented fact that the most important survival skill we can have is simply a well developed ability to think 'What if?' What if X happened? What could you do? What are the things that could go wrong in a kayaking situation that are different from the problems you're used to in your everyday life?

Kayaking *is* my everyday life, so personally I'm more likely to perform an extensive risk assessment about going to the supermarket. But if you're coming at it from a different angle, there are a few basics that I can probably help you with.

If you're not doing anything that's physically strenuous to you, the most likely thing to go wrong is an equipment failure. The two I see happen all the time are so mundane, yet really rather awkward:

1. Leaving the drain plug out of the boat – you wouldn't believe how often this happens. And then, sooner or later, you'll sink.

2. Breaking or losing the paddle and not having a spare.

I don't think I need to go into any more detail about the first mistake. The solution to the second could be to carry a two- or three-piece spare paddle, or to be OK with paddling home with your hands, or being towed home, or leaving your boat and walking... or attaching your paddle to the kayak with a leash. All I need to say is, think about the possible outcomes.

In more adventurous undertakings, the mishaps become necessarily more extreme. Perhaps you could break the kayak. Or lose it. Or head butt a rock and give yourself concussion and a broken nose, teeth and cheekbone. I did that. But much more likely is something like sore wrists, aching shoulders or a bad back. And these ailments can be made much less likely by a bit of simple preparation.

⬆ **One of the most basic safety errors is simply forgetting to close the drain plug on your kayak!**

⬅ **Like many people, I sometimes don't wear a helmet. If I had been wearing one, this wouldn't have happened. Just saying...**

WARM UP AND STRETCH

I never did this when I was younger, and I was injured a lot, and found that after 30 minutes in the boat I was starting to get tired – because I was fighting cold muscles and unyielding tendons. By the time I was properly warmed up it was game over. I was tired from fighting my own body. I thought I was really unfit, but I wasn't. I was just doing it wrong.

It takes ten minutes of gentle exercise like fast walking, jogging, star-jumps or whatever you like, if you're a teenager. If you're middle-aged I'd suggest 30 minutes of even more gentle exercise than that. It's a drag and I never feel like doing it, especially as it cuts into my actual boating time, but it does help a lot. Then do a range of basic stretches on dry land.

Finally, do some rotation and forward and backward stretches in the boat. This has the added advantage of making sure your range of movement in the kayak is unencumbered, and that there's nothing in the boat that's likely to injure you.

Some kayaks, like the hi-tech composite ones made for competition, are extremely light. Most of them aren't. So it's a good idea to have some tricks up your sleeve for carrying them to and from the water.

If your boat is really unwieldy, you can use a trolley to drag it along. But sooner or later you're going to want to lift it. Two people can carry the kayak very easily by holding one end each; but if you know how, you can usually carry one alone. It's just a question of balance.

➡ **A simple kayak trolley helps you trundle around easily, even with a heavy boat.**

⬆ **If you don't want to leave the trolley behind, it's sometimes practical to take it with you on the kayak.**

➡ **Most kayaks can be carried in one hand for short distances, as long as you can hold them at the point of balance.**

The balance point of most kayaks is in the cockpit, where your thighs would go. Sit-on kayaks sometimes have a handle here you can use, or you can just grasp the edge of the cockpit rim. Then you can carry the kayak as if it was a suitcase. A very long suitcase, admittedly.

For longer carries you may prefer to rest the boat on your shoulder. Stand facing the boat, and bend your knees to take hold of the far side of the cockpit with both hands. Then, using your legs as much as possible, straighten up and bring the kayak up to shoulder level with an elbow curl action. Finally, let go with the hand nearer the bow, and turn to put your shoulder into the boat behind the remaining hand.

Whichever method you use, it often helps to stick the paddle into the cockpit right down to the foot area, and use it both as a handle and a shoulder rest. After all, you were going to have to carry it anyway. If it doesn't suit you to do this, however, walk to where you left the paddle on the ground and put your foot carefully under the middle of the shaft. With a little practice you should be able to flick the paddle up with your foot and catch it in your free hand. Very cool.

If it's very windy you'll find the kayak blows around wildly and it's

⬆ **Picking up the paddle with your foot. Always impresses...**

⬆ **Always bend your legs and keep your back straight when lifting a kayak, or anything else heavy.**

➡ **If you have two kayaks to carry it's usually easier to double up as shown here than to struggle with one boat each.**

STORING YOUR KAYAK

Kayaks are best stored as they're transported – on their side or upside down. You can hang them up, or put them on a rack or trestles, but aim to support them about a quarter-way in from each end. Plastic boats especially can be distorted by being supported too close to the centre. In particular, don't store plastic boats right side up on the ground, unless they have a completely flat hull, because they get a flat spot in the middle that wears, and also makes them slow.

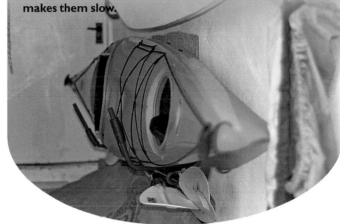

absolutely exhausting to carry it like this. Try pointing it into the wind rather than fighting it. If it's still too difficult, give up and ask someone to help you. It's not worth getting a hernia over.

⬅⬇ **You can tie the boats on with rope, but it's better to use cam-buckle/ratchet straps and then tie off the loose ends of the tape. Never, never use shockcord – it's dangerous and will probably fail.**

TRANSPORTING YOUR KAYAK BY CAR

To transport your boat on the roof of your car you'll need a pretty sturdy roof-rack, and it's best to add padding to the bars – you can buy pads from most kayak shops, or just get pipe insulation from your local DIY store. Two boats can be transported side by side. It's usual to tie them on upside down in case it rains, and because the deck is usually a better shape and less prone to damage than the hull, but it very much depends on the boats' shapes and common sense.

You can get a roof-bar accessory called 'uprights' to carry four or more boats on their sides, which is an even safer way to transport them, or a V-bar, which supports fragile racing kayaks in a right-side-up orientation.

A cockpit cover will improve your fuel economy, keep the noise down and stop unwanted aliens from getting into your boat. It's also useful because you can throw all your wet kit in the boat and put the cover on, instead of putting it in the car!

A lot of serious kayakers prefer to use vans than cars, and if your boats are short enough you can keep them in the back. In mine

I have a raised bed platform and up to four boats can go under the bed, plus more up above in the roof space, because it's very hard work climbing up on the roof to get boats on and off. If you have to, though, because the boats are too long, make sure you use a ladder, get enough assistance, and exercise proper caution. No point in hurting yourself!

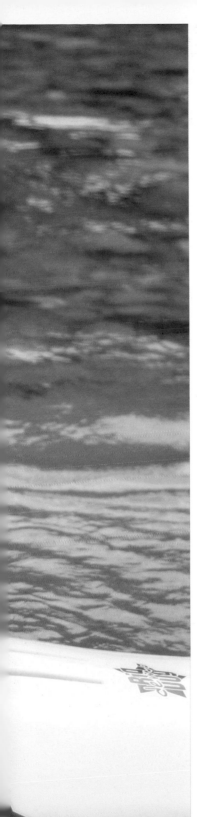

CHAPTER 2

BASIC SKILLS

In the following section we're going to look at the fundamental paddling techniques that are relevant to every kind of kayaking. This is the stuff that's going to make a big difference, and amp your enjoyment of paddling right off the scale. I hope so, anyway...

GETTING IN AND OUT

Getting in and out of a kayak can be a little bit daunting, but it's very easy really. All kayaks have their different issues. Some are very tippy. Some have small cockpits that make wriggling into them a bit tricky. Some are too fragile or precious to be allowed to touch the ground, dock or jetty. But all of these problems can be overcome with a few basic skills.

The first rule of getting into any small boat is, put your weight in the middle so that you don't tip it over. If you can't put your weight in the middle straight away, then you must support it on both sides of the cockpit at the same time.

You can either get into the kayak while it's floating, or get into it on the land and then slide, or be pushed or dragged, into the water. The first is preferable because it causes less wear and tear on both your boat and the environment.

→ **Where possible, place the kayak into deep water so that you don't damage it or leave plastic marks everywhere.**

SIT-ON KAYAK

A sit-on-top kayak is the easiest type to get seated in. With the paddle on the bank, or in the water between you and the kayak so that it can't drift away, plonk your bottom in the seat well, then swing your legs in and put your feet in the most convenient slots that keep a moderate amount of knee bend. Pick up the paddle right away.

→ **The sit-on kayak makes life very easy for us – just jump on and paddle away! If there are two of you, one can steady the kayak while the other gets in. But even alone, it's very easy to keep hold of the bank and your paddle and everything else, because you aren't trying to wriggle into the boat, and it isn't too tippy.**

CLOSED-COCKPIT

With a closed-cockpit kayak the best thing to do is sit astride the back of the boat and then bring your feet into the cockpit and slide your bottom in. If the boat has to be next to a dock or jetty, you may have to stand in the seat first and then sit down on the back deck and proceed from there.

There's a long tradition of teaching people to place the paddle as a bridge from the dock to the back of the cockpit rim, and then slide yourself across this bridge to get in the boat. The idea behind this is good, in that it keeps you connected to the dock as you get in, and supports your weight on the back deck, but I see more people get in a muddle trying to do this than with any other method, and modern paddles are often fragile and unsuited to being used as bridges or seats. So personally I never do it!

If you're wearing a sprayskirt, pull it up to make sure you're not sitting on it as you slide into the cockpit, otherwise you pretty much have to lift yourself up and get in all over again.

The other classic mistake I see a lot is getting into a long boat on a steep beach or slipway pointing directly downhill. As you push yourself into the water, the front of the boat will float but the stern will still be balanced on dry land. At this moment everything becomes extremely wobbly, and many people fall in. It's an OK way to launch a short kayak with rocker, but not a longer boat, especially with a keel.

GETTING OUT OF THE KAYAK

The most important thing to remember is to keep control of your paddle and your kayak at all times. It's all too easy to push them away

→ This is the best way to get into a decked kayak from the beach. Don't try it on a very steep beach or slipway though, because the stern will still be aground while the rest is floating and that's very wobbly indeed!

from you as you regain dry land, with hilarious consequences.

The best way to get out is almost always the exact reverse of how you got in. Sometimes that isn't quite possible, but it's a good principle to work from. Put your paddle on the shore or safely between the kayak and the dock, or parked under shockcords if you have them. Then keep your weight centred in the boat as you get up or out, and make sure you keep hold of the boat and don't kick it away from you as you go.

← Using the paddle as a stabiliser and to stop the kayak floating away, you have both hands free to lift yourself up and sit on the back of the cockpit.

← Get one leg at a time out onto dry land, being careful not to sit on the paddle and crush it!

← Step out of the kayak and pick up the boat and the paddle before they drift away.

FAST WATER EXIT

If the water is moving get out as quickly as possible, keeping hold of everything, and hoist the boat away from the water before anything can get silly.

SITTING CORRECTLY IN YOUR KAYAK

Sitting correctly in your boat is very important, both for health and safety reasons and so that you can paddle it properly for long periods of time.

The first thing to work out is which way round you're supposed to sit. Most boats are pointy at the front and less so at the back, but kayaks can be pretty symmetrical, and it's really funny to watch someone trying to insinuate their legs into the back of one. The shape of the seat and cockpit should give you some clues. Cockpits are normally narrower and higher at the front. Normally.

The next thing to know is how to sit on the seat with your spine upright, but maintaining a good S-shaped spinal posture. The trick is to sit on the edge of your pelvis, not crunched on to the back of it, and to use any back support the boat may have to maintain the bottom half of the curve – known as the lower back lordosis – rather than slumping or leaning back against it.

The position of the legs is also important. In a sit-on kayak, the only important thing is that the legs are comfortable and that they remain slightly bent. In a closed-cockpit boat they should be apart, so that the knees are under the deck or knee hooks/thigh grips, and again, slightly bent but in good contact with the footrest. In an open-cockpit boat like a racing K1 the knees should be up but kept close together.

You may have to mess about with the footrest and back strap for a while before you find the right set-up. This shouldn't be super-tight – you need to be able to relax a bit. But it's surprising how much control you don't have, if you can't brace yourself against the boat properly!

⬆ **The cockpit may or may not have a seat and/or backrest at the rear of it, but it will certainly be narrower at the front than the back, which helps you avoid the novice error of trying to get in the wrong way round!**

⬇ **It's important to sit right back against the backrest and keep the lower part of the spine upright. Slouching isn't just lazy, it's very bad for your back!**

⬇ **Your feet should be braced against any footrest and your legs should be apart so that they are under the deck (of a closed-cockpit boat).**

CAPSIZE DRILL

⬆ **It's not hard to bail out from a sit-on kayak. You pretty much just fall off!**

➡ **Bang your hands on the hull of the boat before you get out. It's a good way to attract attention as soon as possible in case you get stuck.**

➡ **Push yourself out of the cockpit and only when you are sure you are out, twist to the side to get your head above water.**

➡ **Keep hold of the boat and the paddle and wait for assistance if it is available.**

So, you've just got yourself settled in the boat, and are looking forward to a bit of paddling. Bad news. It's really, really super important that you make sure you can get out of the boat if it capsizes. Because it might. So you need to try that next. Make sure that someone competent is on hand to help you if it doesn't go swimmingly, and try it in water that's shallow enough that they can stay on their feet but deep enough that you won't bang your head! It's great if you can practise the first time in a swimming pool or nice warm lagoon.

Sit-on-top paddlers – you're almost excused from this exercise. Sit-on kayaks are almost impossible to capsize, and you shouldn't have any trouble getting out from under one if it did. But I still think you should try it, just so you know what it takes to tip one over, what it feels like when it happens, and so that you have absolutely no fear of it happening again. That will help so much with your paddling.

Closed-cockpit paddlers – you *have* to do it. It isn't safe not to, and you'll probably never paddle properly if you live in fear of capsizing.

Three things are important: that you get out of the boat safely; that you keep control of the kayak and your paddle at all times; and that you don't drown.

For the first attempt, if you have helpers on hand you can try it without the paddle and without your sprayskirt on. But before you set off on your adventures I really do advise that you try executing the whole thing properly. Practise releasing the skirt a few times before you capsize, keeping hold of the paddle with the other hand.

To get out of the boat safely, wait until it's upside down. It's tempting to leap out sooner, but it's safer not to. Trust me. Lean forward, *not* back. Even though you'll want to lean back, *don't*.

Keep hold of the paddle with one hand. Next, bang on the sides of the boat with your other hand to attract attention. That way, if you get stuck somehow help is on its way. Remove your spray skirt, if you're wearing one, by pulling on the handle at the front.

Still leaning forward, put your hands either side of your hips and firmly push away from the seat. Once you're sure your legs are coming free, twist to one side to pop your head up next to the boat. Don't start swimming, just hold the cockpit with your free hand, because the paddle is in the other one. Or should be. Leave the boat upside down.

Regain your composure, then work your way to one end of the boat. Swim it ashore, or await your rescuer. Breathe while you are above the water. Don't breathe while you're under the water. That's my top tip for achieving point number three.

HOLDING AND USING THE PADDLE

It's amazing how many people don't know how to hold the paddle properly, and it's really difficult and tiring to propel and manoeuvre a kayak if you don't. I'm going to keep this quite short and punchy:

The right grip-width is such that if you put the paddle on your head, your elbows would make right angles, as shown in the photo.

Your hands should both be the same distance from the centre of the shaft, or the same distance from the ends.

If you're paddling with a cranked shaft, you should be holding the part of the crank that's angled back towards the stern. See the photo. You don't have a choice about grip width in this instance, so you'd better hope the paddle is the right length for you!

If your paddle is right-handed you should hold it with your right hand so that the drive face of the right blade is upright and facing the stern when your right arm is outstretched, as per the photo. This is your control hand – the other hand should grip loosely so that the paddle can turn in it. If your paddle is left-handed, replace all the 'rights'

in the preceding sentences with 'lefts'. It doesn't matter at this point whether you're right- or left-handed, by the way. If you've got to this point and you're holding a right-handed paddle, you're paddling right-handed. Deal with it.

If the blade is asymmetric, the shorter, cut-away bit of the blade should be at the bottom. If it isn't, turn the whole paddle round left to right and that will fix it.

The whole left- or right-handed control hand situation works like this. Most paddles have feather, an offset angle between the blades that helps keep wind and water resistance to a minimum. This means that you have to make a little twist with your hands each time you put a blade in the water, to make sure it goes in nice and vertical. The control hand does the twist, and the other hand lets the shaft turn.

Try to make each stroke deep enough that the whole blade is immersed, but don't put it in so far that your hand gets wet. Keep the blades as close to the boat as is convenient without scraping.

⬇ **This is the correct place to hold a cranked shaft, and places your wrists at a less stressful angle.**

➔ **With your arms stretched straight out in front of you, the paddle blade on the control hand side should be upright.**

ACTION AND REACTION

One of the things that people find confusing, when they first start paddling, is that the balance and motion skills we all learn as a child don't really work the same way in a kayak. Most kayaks are unusually small and responsive boats, so the body language of the paddler has a big effect. And very often this effect is the opposite of what is expected.

It's very difficult to 'unlearn' the skills you've acquired through years of just walking around, but if you practise the actions that make the boat do what you want it to, you should eventually reprogramme yourself.

As you can see from the diagram, the kayak has three planes of movement. If the bow rises or falls, that's called 'pitch'. Turning to the left or right is called 'yaw'. And the one that people think about the most, tipping from side to side? We call that 'roll'.

When beginners are worried that they're going to capsize in a kayak, they respond with an instinct that's called 'reflex balance'. In most human experience you can stop yourself falling to the left by trying to lean to the right. Sometimes that's accompanied by a bit of waving the arms about. In a kayak, this response will do exactly the opposite of what you wanted. Because you're sitting down, and any body movement is achieved by bending from the hips, by trying to bend to the right you'll actually be rolling the boat to the left. And you're holding a paddle, which tends to stop you using your arms the way you'd normally do to keep your balance.

It's going to take a little while to stop reacting this way, but the best advice for beginners is: if you think you're going to capsize, put your paddle on that side and try to lean that way also. OK, you did it too late, after doing the wrong lean first? Of course you did. Just keep it in mind, and it'll become normal eventually.

I really want to keep the science lessons to a minimum, but it's a good idea at this point to understand a thing that's sometimes called 'swing weight'. If you want to rotate something, two things matter. How heavy it is, and how far that weight is distributed from the axis. Kayaks generally weigh a lot less than people, so they're easier to rotate. That's why, when you try to twist your body to the right, it pretty much stays where it was and the boat twists the opposite way instead. The same thing happens in the yaw plane. Hold your paddle in front of you, and then rotate to the left and the boat will start to turn to the right. If it's a short boat, this will be quite dramatic. In a long touring or racing boat, it

will be very slight, because the longer boat has more yaw plane swing weight as well as more drag in the water.

In the pitch plane, there are two different effects. Static and dynamic. If you lean forward very slowly, the bow of the kayak will sink slightly, as you might expect. But if you lean forward quickly you actually pull the bow up towards you. Then it sinks back down, after bobbing up and down a bit maybe. Leaning back follows the same pattern, but doesn't make so much difference usually, because you can't move your centre of gravity back as far as you can forward. It's just a physiological fact when you're sitting in a kayak with your legs in front of you.

Anyway, this is useful to know and to understand. Why? Because even quite experienced paddlers often try to 'react' to the front of the boat purling by leaning back, but they do it too suddenly and make things worse. Just like the roll-plane reflex balance thing, it's good to keep reminding yourself of what's actually going to happen when you move your body.

⬆ **The correct way to react if the boat tips and you don't want it to: keep your weight firmly on the side you are tipping towards and lean on your paddle.**

⬆ **The wrong way to react – but what most beginners do. Don't try to lean away from the water, it makes matters worse!**

⬆ **This paddler fears the worst and leans back to try to keep the bow up. As you can see, it doesn't.**

⬆ **This paddler has kept their weight nicely centred and has kept the bow dry and under control.**

PADDLING THE KAYAK

The most important thing to learn is how to make the kayak move through the water efficiently. The problem that most people have is making it go in a straight line. What I've always said to complete beginners is this: the simple rule is to make big wide arcs with the paddle only when you want to turn the boat, but use very vertical, close to the hull strokes when you want to go straight. As soon as the boat starts to veer one way, make the next stroke on that side a wide sweep to catch it.

That's probably all you need to know to have a go and get around your local pond, but serious paddlers want a more developed and efficient technique. Most people become aware pretty quickly that it's a good idea to utilise more muscles than just your arms, and a great deal has been written in the past about using a pedalling action with the legs to try to add power to the stroke, blah blah blah. It sounds a bit suspicious while not completely ridiculous. I believed it for ages, but now I think this: unless you actually swivel on your seat, or have a swivelling seat the way some race boats do, I don't see how 'pedalling' can give you much extra. In fact I've tried pedalling versus non-pedalling, and I've tried pushing with the water-blade leg versus pushing with the air-blade leg, and I can't tell much difference. Nor can my stopwatch.

However, that's not to say that the leg muscles don't come into play. They very much do. But concentrate on your upper body and your legs will do what they have to do to make that happen – there's no need to confuse yourself with pedalling until you aspire to be an Olympic racer. Engage the core and use body rotation to extend the stroke and factor in many more muscle groups.

I said extend the stroke. The name of the game is to make the effective length of the stroke as long as possible. And the key word there is 'effective'. If you reach forward too far with the paddle, the blade goes into the water at a very inclined angle and clearly doesn't deliver much power until it's closer to upright. In fact what it does is deliver pitch energy, lifting the bow out of the water, which is effort wasted. The same applies at the end of the stroke. Once the paddle is very inclined it's scooping up water and fighting gravity, and delivering a bunch of yaw and roll force as well, probably.

So massive body rotation allows you to make the stroke longer while keeping the paddle fairly upright.

You can test out how well this strategy works by trying to paddle with your arms locked straight. That's not actually a really good way to paddle, but it's a good exercise, because after you get over moaning that it feels weird and wondering if everyone is thinking you look like an idiot (they aren't, get over yourself) it actually turns out to be surprisingly practical. In fact the interesting thing for me is that straight-arm paddling (ie taking your arms almost completely out of the equation) seems to deliver about 90% as much power as using them for most of your motive force – which is in stark contrast to the pedalling experiment. Once you can do it, relax your elbows a bit to be more natural.

It's all a bit counter-intuitive, huh? But if you try paddling with your arms locked straight for a bit you'll start to feel the sense of it. That'll also get your body rotating, which is about ten times more powerful than what you can do with your arms, because it's driven by your quads. Quads? What? But sir, I thought you said the legs didn't do anything? No, I didn't say that. I said actively pedalling with them doesn't do anything. But much of the upper body movement you can achieve while sitting in a boat is powered by your legs, even if those legs can't move at all. Your abs and biceps deliver fine control along with all those muscles in your back that have cute Latin names but nobody cares about, and the major motive power comes from the shoulders, triceps and quads.

← **Paddling with your arms completely straight is not quite the way forward, but it does teach you how to rotate your body to move the paddle blade through the stroke.**

FEEDBACK

I read something about this a long time ago, and didn't think much about it until I was talking to a top swimmer, who said that awareness of feedback from the power surfaces (hands, arms and legs in the case of a swimmer) is of critical importance in getting the most out of an already good stroke. For a paddler it's the same, except that our power surface – the blade – is bigger and on the end of a long stick.

This introduces a whole bunch of issues, but the main one is that we have to interpret the feedback that comes to us as twisting forces and/or pressure differences between our two hands. Some people are naturally better at this than others. These people are called kinaesthetic learners by some, and lucky gits by almost everyone else; but in fact we can all benefit from what nature has given a few of us, by simply sticking a blade in the water and wiggling it around. Try it. Just sit somewhere quiet for half an hour, put a blade in the water and move it around. For ages. If you think you aren't learning anything, then keep doing it until you do. Then change sides, because there would be no point in magically improving your paddling skill on one side only, you'd just go round in circles. And I'm pretty sure that investing a little time in, let's call it 'stirring', will pay dividends when it comes to the intricacies of advanced strokes.

PUSH OR PULL?

It depends on your paddling background and experience, but most people still think of forward paddling as pulling the blade through the water. But watch any trained racer and you will see that the opposite is true. Most of the force is *push*, and the water blade is the pivot.

I've tried to compare it with planting a ski stick, or with pole vaulting, but these are pretty weak analogies. The best I can come up with is poling a boat, in the manner of a Venetian gondolier, or a student on the Cam. Would you rather plant a stick into the riverbed in front of you and try to pull yourself towards it, or would you plant it behind you and use it as a fulcrum? Does the latter seem so much more efficient and ergonomic that you'd scarcely bother to incorporate the former strategy into the equation? Thought so... same for paddling, then. Concentrate on punching/pushing with your top arm, and keep the water blade elbow almost locked out to make the best use of the leverage. Never actually pull with the bottom arm unless you're trying to turn. Any pulling force comes from rotating your body and engaging your abs and lats.

← **Excellent paddling style: rotate your shoulders and push with your top hand, and you will go faster and further than you could before. The elbow bend is just to recover the blade at the end of the stroke and set you up for the next 'punch'.**

↑ **Even in the midst of all this rough water and turbulence, a skilful paddler can hold the paddle with a light and hence sensitive grip.**

GORILLA GRIP

For thousands of years we've been pretty smug about having opposable thumbs, and I always assumed that they were pretty much essential for paddling. I confess, I spent a lot of my kayaking career clinging on to my paddle with a vice-like grip, convinced that if it was wrenched from my grasp I'd have to swim and subsequently drown. Only much later did I learn that by gripping the paddle tightly we actually lock out a lot of muscles and functionality in the arms, and severely hamper our ability to exercise fine control. Nowadays I almost never engage my thumbs at all, and just keep them in readiness to close my grip if the river tries to take the paddle away from me.

HIGH OR LOW ANGLE?

This one's a bit more complicated. We can't just look at the racers for inspiration. While they tend always to paddle with a very high angle, there are sometimes other things to consider – the design of your boat, for one. A racehead paddling style doesn't work well in a wide whitewater boat, for instance. The angle needs to come down a bit to stop the upper body waggling around from side to side to a degree that negatively impacts on general smoothness; and sometimes because the water can be shallow, and running over your blade with the boat on the approach to a waterfall can lead to disappointment. Or in a sea kayak a very high style can catch too much wind, and doesn't allow enough margin for absorbing hull roll from waves.

Paddle design can make a difference too. Long, thin paddle blades like Greenland sticks and some other sea-specific paddles just feel wrong in the very high registers of stroke angle that work really well with a 'Euro' style blade. What should we do about that? Well, if all else fails I reckon we should moderate the high style a bit, because what we lose that way is less than what's lost from the aforementioned goings-wrong.

There is, however, a technique that can help with directional stability issues, which are a common cause of low, inefficient paddling full of adjustments and steering strokes.

A LITTLE EXTRA MAGIC

I'm ashamed to say that I discovered this only about two years ago, after several decades of paddling... well, everything. For a while I said nothing, assuming everyone else knew about it already and that it had been blind luck that I'd got by all that time without getting busted for a rank amateur. But then I slipped it cunningly into conversation and was met with blank looks all around. And after checking for hidden cameras, I decided it was time to go public. So here it is. It's a trick that works in kayaks, canoes, or on a stand-up paddleboard. Probably the effects are more noticeable in the latter two, but it's jolly useful in a kayak too, especially one that doesn't like to go in a straight line.

Here it is. While paddling normally, make a slight adjustment to the angle of the paddle blade in the water as viewed from above: 2° to 5° will do. You can do this by changing your grip or by just rotating your wrist a bit. I call this 'canting' the blade one way or the other. See what happens.

OK, that's a bit boring unless you have the book in your boat right now, so I'll tell you what happens. If you have the feedback/stirring skills to make a stroke like this without changing the path of the blade – in other words without slicing – the boat will be moved sideways.

Now, it isn't a big mental leap to see that you can use this effect to stop the boat from turning away from the paddle, a big problem in directionally unstable kayaks, for instance playboats. Turn the drive face in a few degrees for the first half of the stroke, and Bob's your uncle. If you need tons of steering compensation, cant in for the first half, and out for the second half – which is very similar to what canoe paddlers call a J-stroke. But it'll only work if you have a 'feel' for the blade in the water and maintain positive pressure without messing up the path of the paddle. This you can do, if you've spent a lot of time 'stirring' – or are some sort of kinaesthetic genius.

PADDLING BACKWARDS

You know the first thing people always do? Turn the paddle around in their hands so that they can paddle backwards still using the drive face. It's not silly, it's the obvious thing to do if you haven't been told otherwise. I get that. But it's wrong. Firstly because we never (usually)

↑ **The low stroke angle is still better with a Greenland stick, or a very long touring paddle.**

⬆ **Beginners usually use the paddle at a lower angle, but so do smaller people or users of wide boats no matter how great their experience.**

⬆ **But the more vertical paddle is the hallmark of the expert paddler in most cases.**

change our grip on the paddle, since that opens a whole can of worms when you need a normal grip right afterwards; but mostly because paddling backwards with the back face of the blade actually works a whole lot better. Why, I really couldn't say, but it may be something to do with the curvature of the blade suiting the rather different stroke ergonomics our bodies produce in that mode.

So, *don't* turn the paddle round. I think you got that part. But do rotate your body to place the blade in the water behind you at the start of your stroke, and as you do so take a quick look behind you to see where you're going.

You won't be able to paddle at a stylishly high angle with a reverse stroke, but make them pushy strokes if you can rather than big wide sweeps. Most of the control for this seems to come from the elbows. It's very much *not* the reverse of paddling forwards, but a quite different style. You may find it hard to go straight in some types of boats, but like anything it comes with practice.

Think before you back-paddle. In many short or manoeuvrable kayaks it may well be quicker and easier just to turn the boat around and paddle forwards.

⬆ **Paddling smoothly backwards in a sea kayak.**

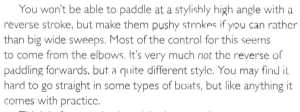

⬆ **Always look behind you every few strokes when back-paddling.**

FORWARD SWEEP STROKE

As I explained in the section about forward paddling, the boat is easier to keep moving in a straight line if you make your strokes close and parallel to the side of the kayak, and the best way to do this is to have quite a high-angle paddling style. However, when you need to make a steering correction it works well to sweep the paddle in a lower, wider arc, which will turn the bow away from the paddle. This is pretty simple to incorporate and most people have it down in a few minutes – especially if they're paddling a slalom boat or round-hulled general-purpose kayak. Because until you've mastered what I'm talking about, you just go round in circles.

The forward sweep stroke, as this technique is usually known, is so important and useful that it's worth spending a bit of time going through it in more detail. It's not only a stroke for correcting the track of an errant kayak on the move; it's also the most powerful stroke for rotating the boat when standing still.

The most effective part of this stroke is the beginning. Put the paddle blade in the water as far forward as you can, with the drive face

away from the hull. Your reach is enhanced by keeping the paddle shaft low in this stroke. Next, sweep the blade away from the kayak, in as wide an arc as you can manage without feeling wobbly. Go right round in a semicircle, and you should find that the boat, too, has rotated up to 180°. Make sure you lift the blade out of the water well before it hits the stern of the kayak. Otherwise, sploosh – you fall in.

Once you're feeling confident with doing that on both sides, try to do it while you're moving along. You can change direction quite suddenly without losing any speed. I find in most boats that it's best just to do the first half of the stroke, and then morph it back into a normal power stroke, because there seems to be a diminishing return after the blade passes the midpoint when you're moving. Also, try making the arc even bigger by leaning your weight on to the paddle. It may help to feather the paddle a little so the drive face points a little down, to give you more support. Or you may just fall in. But nothing ventured, nothing gained. And depending on your boat, you might want to lean the boat along with your body (sea kayak or other keeled boat), or try to keep it flat (planing hull kayak or some other flattish designs).

REVERSE SWEEP STROKE

The reverse version of the sweep stroke is, surprisingly enough, the exact reverse of the forward sweep. It's equally powerful when stationary, but when moving forward it clearly causes quite a lot of drag and slows you, often to a standstill. But maybe that's what you need. How am I to know?

Of course, when you're moving backwards the reverse sweep is the best way to make corrections while maintaining speed. But it's hard to start it right at the stern, so despite what we learnt with the forward sweep, it's often the latter part of the stroke that's effective at speed. At a stop though, the further back you can reach, the more turning force you'll have.

For spinning a longer boat around, it's good to do a forward sweep on one side, then a reverse sweep on the other, and keep alternating like that until you're pointing the way you want to be. If you're paddling the sort of boat that benefits from a big lean to release the rails or keel, this might imply that you need to flop around from one side to the other like a mad person, so it's worth having a go at keeping the boat leaning over one way, while still alternating the strokes. I think I'd generally lean towards my forward sweep, and then would be leaning away from the reverse... but it very much depends on your boat and your balance. Try everything, and see how you get on!

TO EDGE OR TO LEAN?

If you lean over to one side you'll eventually need to learn how to support your weight using the paddle, to stop you from falling over. Luckily I'm going to explain that a little further on. What I want to explain here is that you can lean your body over without tipping the boat, but that doesn't help much to release your edges or keel from the water. You can, however, lean over and keep the boat at the same angle as your body. That's what we usually refer to as 'leaning'. But there's a third scenario, wherein you tip the boat using your knees or hips and keep your body upright. This is called 'edging'. Clearly, this can give you the hydrodynamic effect you're looking for without the wobbly situation you're trying to avoid.

TURNING THE BOAT BY LEANING OR EDGING

It's at about this time in the skills acquisition process that I like to mention the fact that you often don't need to use strokes to turn the boat. Most boats respond to lean or edge. The confusing thing is that it's a dynamic not a static effect, so it depends on what else is going on.

Broadly speaking, if the boat is moving forwards and you give it a bit of tilt, whether by edging or leaning, it will probably begin to turn. However, some boats turn on an inside lean, like a bicycle or a skateboard, and some turn on an outside lean, like, well, a kayak actually. Many boats will be equally happy to turn with either, and depend very much on subtle forces like which side you made the last stroke, or wind or current. So I find the best thing to do until you've really started to make friends with the boat is to help the turn with a little touch of forward sweep stroke as you start the lean, just to make sure it knows which way to turn.

In most boats, an outside edge or an inside lean are a safe bet to make the turn, whether they're displacing or planing. With just a little confident touch from the paddle you can make that turn a lot more elegantly than it would have been if you'd just stayed bolt upright and heaved on a blade.

⬆ **Edging – the body stays in the upright position and the boat is tipped to one side.**

⬅ **In a lean, the body is at the same roll angle as the boat.**

STOPPING

Clearly, having learned to move your boat through the water at a reasonable pace, it's important to understand how to stop it as well – usually in order to avoid a collision. I can't think of any other good reason right now.

There's a very standardised way of stopping a kayak which is covered in most books and other instructional media. I'm going to take you through it step by step, but before I do I want to explain that it's not the best or only way to stop a kayak, and it's not the way skilful paddlers would use if they could help it.

The principle is simple – while moving forwards, you jab the paddle into the water and try to resist as the water carries it backwards, as shown in the photo sequence. This clearly slows the boat down, but it also makes it turn towards the paddle, so you respond to that by jabbing it in on the other side as well, with the same result, and then back to the first side, until you're stationary or even moving backwards.

As I say, that's the textbook way to stop a kayak quickly. But it's rubbish. It feels rubbish. It also looks inelegant, and you'll probably nearly tip yourself over the first time you try it. So for me, it's the absolute last resort.

The best way to stop depends on two things: the type of boat you're paddling, and the type of water you're paddling on.

In a short and easy-turning kind of boat, one of the best ways to stop is to let it slew sideways, a bit like a skier or a snowboarder skidding to a halt. But less dramatic. The boat won't carry much momentum through the turn, especially if you turn on a low brace or a bow rudder. It will just turn 90° and stop.

This works with longer boats too, but they tend to carry a bit more speed, and you might be grumpy about turning if that's not the direction you wanted to be going. So in a longer boat consider putting down the paddle and sticking both hands in the water as brakes, or, wherever possible, simply going around the obstacle instead of stopping.

Surfing a wave? Turn sideways, or capsize, or ender if the wave has a breaking component that would carry a boat sideways.

On a rapid ? Catch an eddy, park on a shoal or flat rock. Think outside the box!

← ↙ Digging in the paddle blade repetitively on either side of the boat is the standard way to stop, but it's clumsy and splashy.

↓ Allow the boat to slew sideways. Clearly, it's going to stop almost instantly.

STERN STROKES

Beginners usually work out that if they drag the paddle or dig it in on one side while moving along, it turns the boat towards the paddle. However, it's a noisy and unsatisfying way to turn, and slows you down.

A more subtle way to do it is to trail the paddle on the surface of the water, back face downwards, and then lean on it gently. This is called a low brace turn, and it's the one to fall back on when you're feeling a bit challenged and want to be very stable in your turn. However, it still slows you down, and that might not be what you want.

⬆ **The intuitive way beginners try to turn a kayak. As you can see, it's a lot of effort and it doesn't really work.**

⬇ **The low brace turn is a much more elegant way of executing the manoeuvre, especially when combined with the right amount of lean for your kayak.**

It's what you want if you're paddling up to a dock with the intention of coming to a halt next to it. Paddle gently, straight towards the jetty or whatever, and then just before the bow gets there, apply a low brace turn. You'll find it surprisingly easy to time things just right, so that you turn 90° and end up stationary right beside your chosen landing place.

⬆ Usually the best way to approach a side-on landing/docking situation, especially if the water is too shallow to bow rudder or draw stroke. Oops... I haven't mentioned those yet. Read on!

⬆ Trailing the blade edge on as a rudder allows you to carry more speed through the turn.

⬇↘ If you want to increase the steering force or turn it into a stopping manoeuvre, try sweeping the blade smoothly out and forward.

So the next development is to trail the paddle blade behind you, but with the blade upright as shown. Try to rotate your body enough so that the paddle shaft is actually parallel to the side of the boat. My other hot tip is, don't be lazy and rest it on the deck. Look at the rear blade and make sure it's fully immersed in the water. It shouldn't be doing much – it's like a rudder that no one has turned yet. For this reason it's called a 'stern rudder'. To apply some rudder, push the back blade gently away from the boat while you're still moving. This will make the boat turn towards the paddle, but not slow you down much. Remember, it's a rudder, not a brake.

Incidentally, you can also make the boat turn the other way by pulling the rudder back towards you, but you run a big risk of tripping over it if it hits the boat, so it's usually much better to take it out of the water and apply a stern rudder on the other side if that's the way you need to turn.

These types of steering strokes are easy to learn and to practise, but you'll probably find them superseded pretty quickly by the infinitely cooler and rather more powerful bow steering strokes. However, the stern steers are very useful when you're surfing a wave, being towed, or accelerating down a steep section of rapids, so don't skimp on practising them – they have their place!

→ One classic use of the stern rudder is to steer while surfing a wave.

→ Notice the straight back arm to maintain the rudder near the back of the kayak, and that the front arm is bent to bring the entire paddle across to that side of the boat.

BASIC SKILLS 51

BOW STROKES

Bow steering strokes are by far the most difficult of all strokes to perform, and by the same token I think they're the most satisfying. They're also the most useful and versatile, because they can be combined to move the kayak in any motion, while providing support, without taking the paddle out of the water at all!

You may find it difficult, initially, to make a stroke like this work. It relies on a lot of feedback, and it's a bit weird at first. It's a genuinely advanced stroke, and for this reason you won't see most 'have-a-go' kayakers even attempt it, but watch any expert kayaker and it can sometimes seem as if they use bow strokes to do everything.

Here's how to try it. While paddling forward at your normal cruising speed, next place the blade in the water at 90° to the normal orientation so that the drive face is towards the boat, and just hold it there. It should be about 30cm (12in) from the side of the boat somewhere next to your feet, and if you've understood me it should be slicing through the water as you move forward, with no effect on the boat at all. Next, roll your wrists back to turn the drive face slightly to the bow, and resist the resulting force on the paddle. You can let the water push the blade back a bit, but not too much. Resist, but smoothly. The boat will start to turn smoothly towards the paddle. The more you open the blade angle out, the more you'll turn, but it will also slow you down, so subtle is best.

⬆ **Place the blade in the water near your feet...**

⬆ **...then roll your wrists outwards (turning the drive face towards the bow a bit).**

⬆ **Feel the water pressure push it back a little way...**

⬆ **...but don't let it come further back than your knees.**

↙ **Whitewater kayakers often seem to do everything with bow rudders – because they can, and the blade is always in the water ready to carry on paddling.**

➡ **For maximum effect, start to pull the paddle back into the start position as the move plays out.**

Try to keep your top arm below eye level, partly because that puts less strain on your shoulders but also because it helps with seeing stuff. Try also to lean forward with your body, to keep the blade about level with your feet. You can do this with just your arms, but then the blade angle is less efficient, so it's better to lean forward so that you can keep the paddle fairly upright.

The classic mistake is not to hold the paddle firmly in position relative to the boat. Many beginners turn the boat towards the paddle, and then run over the paddle, trip themselves up and fall in!

Don't be discouraged if your bow rudder doesn't seem to work at first. It takes a bit of practice to get the feel for it, and it takes a fair amount of strength and mobility to make the best of the stroke, but once you've done it you'll love it.

THE BOW DRAW

The bow draw is a variation that can work even if you aren't moving forwards. Simply create the pressure on the drive face by pulling the paddle blade towards the boat, instead of rotating it with your wrists. The kayak will turn just as it did for a bow rudder. Be careful not to keep pulling until it hits the side of the boat, or you'll fall over.

If you've practised 'stirring' as described earlier, you'll be able to do a bow draw and then slice the paddle away from the kayak and repeat, so you can spin the boat around on the spot. The further forward you

reach with the paddle, the more effective this will be.

If you're moving you can do a bow draw to increase the response speed of your bow rudder, or simply to make a subtle change of direction without causing any drag.

⬇ **This is how the bow draw turns the kayak by moving the bow sideways, even without any forward speed.**

If you're paddling a sea kayak or any long boat with a keel, you'll find that leaning the boat over so that the keel releases from the water makes your bow steering much easier. You get quite a lot of support from the paddle too, so don't be afraid to commit a bit of weight to it.

If, on the other hand, you're trying it in a flat-bottomed or very manoeuvrable craft, it may be better to keep the boat dead flat – leaning it over might engage the rails at the sides and make it harder to turn.

↖⬆ **Start as per the bow rudder but with the blade quite far out from the feet, or allow the water to take it there. Then squeeze it smoothly back towards the hull, pulling the front of the boat towards the blade.**

⬇ **In white water the bow draw is a great way of pulling yourself onto the right line while still carrying some momentum.**

SIDEWAYS MOTION

One of many wonderful things about kayaks is that you can move them sideways through the water with your paddle, and that's as deeply satisfying to the paddler as it is mystifying to the uninitiated observer. Which is always fun.

There are two ways to do this. Well, there are three, but I just don't think the third one counts. They are: the draw stroke, the sculling draw, and the sculling push.

Now, I think the sculling push is silly because it's just a sculling draw on the other side of the boat, and it's only useful if you're too close/shallow to use a sculling draw – in which case you could just reach out with your hands and pull yourself in. So, if you anticipate wanting to sneak up sideways to a bramble bush or an electric fence, go ahead and learn the sculling push.

THE DRAW STROKE

Place the paddle vertically in the water as far away from you as you can without falling in, drive face towards the kayak. Now bring your top hand towards you a little, and then start pulling with the bottom hand too – directly towards the side of the boat. Before it hits the hull, turn the blade 90° with your wrists and slice it away from the kayak. This action should have pulled you sideways, but it probably will be more of an angled, crablike motion, because you need to know two more things.

Where the stroke needs to take place along the long axis of the boat depends on where the kayak's centre of pressure lies. If it's a slalom kayak, that's somewhere under your knees. A sea kayak, under the seat. A playboat or creek boat, somewhere in between. And a racing K1, it may even be behind you. Now, at a rough guess I'm going to say that your draw stroke needs to take place halfway between the centre of pressure and your personal centre of gravity, which is maybe 20cm (8in) in front of your belly button. I've made that sound very technical, but it's just something to think about. What I actually do is start the stroke, and see which end of the boat seems to be leading. Then I can move the stroke towards the bow or the stern to compensate. That really isn't too difficult. And sometimes you actually want the boat to crab or turn a bit as you move it, so that's handy.

The other thing you need to know is about lean. It's natural to lean towards the paddle a bit as you do a draw stroke, but in some boats that doesn't help. It does in sea kayaks and similar touring boats that have keel-like shapes at the end, but flat-bottomed boats are better kept flat, and in some boats, like racing K1s, slalom boats or anything with a wide hull and low decks, it may even help to lift the edge on the paddle side to reduce drag. Feels weird, but looks pretty cool, luckily.

THE SCULLING DRAW

Put the paddle vertically in the water as before, and bring your top arm in a bit, as before. Now, instead of pulling, begin slicing the paddle to and fro (along the long axis of the kayak) maybe 30cm (12in), and on each slice use your wrists to angle the leading edge of the blade out slightly so that it tries to move away from the boat. I'm talking about 10–20° of angle. But of course, it can't move away from the boat, because you're holding it, so what it actually does is drag the boat sideways through the water with each slice. The tricky part is that each time you change the direction of the sweep you need to use your wrists to change the blade angle. Leading edge becomes trailing edge every time. The other tricky part is holding your arms quite firm in every other direction while you're moving them to and fro. Calls for a bit of isometric tension.

THE SCULLING PUSH

Is feeble, as I mentioned earlier, but if you must try it, all you need to do is change one thing. Make the leading edge of each slice of the paddle angled in towards the boat, the exact opposite of the draw, and of course the stroke will push the boat sideways away from the paddle. But why you'd want to do that is a mystery to me.

⬆ While sculling the paddle to and fro like this, you need to hold the blade firm and not let it move away from the boat. The more vertical the paddle shaft can be the better. As long as you don't fall over the blade.

HERE'S A GREAT EXAMPLE OF HOW THE MORE ADVANCED STROKES ALL WORK NICELY TOGETHER, AS A PADDLER APPROACHES A LANDING PLACE

⬆ The kayaker approaches paddling normally...

⬆...uses a draw stroke to pull the boat towards the dock...

⬆...a perpendicular rudder/brace to control the approach...

⬆...and finally takes hold of dry land having parked neatly next to it.

SUPPORT STROKES

Another thing that separates a paddler from a dabbler is being able to use the paddle for balance. As I've mentioned elsewhere, body language 'reflex' balancing is counter-productive, but even good body language is pretty feeble unless you have some grip on the water. That connection should come from the paddle.

Now, I'm going to tell you about the few different support strokes that have names, but before I do let me say this: all strokes are support strokes. If your paddle is in the water and you're putting some pressure on one of the faces, then it'll support some of your weight, no matter what the orientation of said paddle might be. It's just that some strokes are more supportive than others. You can learn a lot about this by practising stirring, which I've already mentioned earlier (page 43).

The second thing I want you to remember is that there's a whole bunch of difference between enough support to support you, and enough support to push yourself back upright again. So while you might use a support stroke to stop yourself capsizing any further, the way to right yourself from that position is to use the magic body language that many boaters call a 'hip flick' or 'hip rotation'. Which will be explained in due course.

So, here are the strokes, in the order that might be best to learn them in:

LOW BRACE

Put the paddle in the sort of position you might expect at the end of a normal paddling action, with the back face flat on the water somewhere behind your hips and the shaft as low as can be. Your air-blade hand might be somewhere just above your knee, I'd hypothesise.

If you're moving forward, this is the natural stroke placement. It's just like the low brace turn. However, the further out the water blade is from the boat, the more support you'll get from it, but the harder

it'll be to get your weight back over the boat afterwards. So that's a matter of compromise, and feeling your way.

Also, the faster the boat is moving forwards or the current is flowing under the blade, the more support you'll have. And this doesn't have a downside, which is a rare thing. What I'd mention, though, is that I wouldn't recommend doing this stroke while travelling backwards. Or on the upstream side of the boat. That will end very badly indeed.

So, knowing all these things, lean on the paddle blade. Keep your elbows bent, and keep them above the paddle shaft. When you've put as much weight on it as you dare, or it starts sinking, level the boat using only your hips and legs and leaving your torso where it is. And then simply lift the weight of your upper body and arms off the blade, and carry on with your day.

It's pretty scary at first – all support strokes are a leap of faith. They give you exactly the amount of support that you commit to them, and not a minuscule measure of energy more. Having said that, the low brace may not be the most powerful of support strokes, but it's the one most people default to when things get really wobbly and their confidence is compromised.

HIGH BRACE

A high brace is just like a low brace, but you put the paddle blade drive-face down on the water. It tends to work to do this at about 90° to the boat or even further in front of you, instead of behind (and so you *can* do this while moving backwards). This orientation forces you to have your elbows below the shaft, so you're kind of hanging from it. Unless you're a gibbon, or you've changed your grip on the paddle. In the latter case, you aren't doing a high brace, you're doing a low brace with your paddle upside down. Stop messing about. In the former case, you aren't going to enjoy kayaking, but well done with the reading.

A high brace is more powerful, but it's dangerous, because if it gets overextended by the force of the water it can push your shoulder joint into a weak position or even dislocate it. For this reason a lot of people say don't do it, use a low brace instead. I say, a low brace won't work in extreme degrees of roll, so it's worth having the high brace in your bag of tricks; but don't do it when massive forces are at work, and always try to keep the shaft close in to your chest.

↑ **Even with a narrow Greenland paddle you can commit a lot of weight to a high brace, but with your elbows below shoulder level and your arms in front.**

→ **This is how a high brace goes bad. It's overextended, and the arms are too high, so there's serious risk of injury (anterior shoulder dislocation).**

SCULLING FOR SUPPORT

OK, this is a weird one. And really difficult to describe, so bear with me. The sculling action, as described in the 'sculling draw', is that of sweeping the paddle to and fro, and using the wrists to angle the leading edge of the blade up slightly to help it generate lift or force, a bit like a wing. Well, a bit like the way you might imagine a wing works. The tricky part is that each time you change the direction of the sweep you need to use your wrists to change the blade angle. Leading edge becomes trailing edge at that moment. Clear as mud? Thought so – so look at the pictures.

Now you can scull for support at quite extreme angles, so if you absolutely mustn't capsize, it's a good skill to have. Once you're hanging from the paddle, though, the recovery is basically a roll.

Sculling support works well in long narrow kayaks, but is a bit of a challenge in short wide ones. A lot of people are taught to lie back while sculling, but I prefer to do it with my body at 90° to the kayak. It seems much more powerful to me and complements the way I prefer to roll.

HANGING DRAW

The most powerful support stroke of all is the hanging draw, if you can do it right. It's only safe to do it in front of you, because of the anterior dislocation risk as per the high brace, so in reality what you're doing is committing your weight to a bow draw. Therefore I entreat you to go and learn the bow draw first, as described on page 53, and then practise committing more and more weight to it. The secret of using it as a support stroke is that the support you receive is only as much as the force with which you pull it towards the boat. Angling it out into a high brace position doesn't make it better – the high brace is a less powerful stroke. Just keep messing about with bow draws and stirring until you trust it. It'll come in time.

The most awesome thing about the hanging draw support stroke is that, in time, you'll find you spend much of your paddling time in that bow rudder/draw position, so it's in a way the least inconvenient stroke to make in a pinch.

⬆ Scull the paddle smoothly fore and aft, concentrating on raising the leading edge of the water blade as shown. You can support yourself at any angle. If you have enough faith.

⬇ Hanging draw with a Greenland paddle.

ROLLING AND HOW TO DO IT

Rolling is integral to most people's perceptions of a kayaker. At least, it was until the popularity of the sit-on-top kayak. To the non-boater, it's still the thing that separates a 'have-a-go' paddler from the real deal, and is regarded as something of a black art, a magic trick that follows on from an eventuality that was unthinkable in the first place – capsizing into freezing cold water in a craft from which there's seemingly no escape.

What there is, in the kayaking world, is a good deal of disagreement and misinformation about the best way to roll or learn to roll, and the variety and importance of the different types of roll that one can learn. And I'm not going to say that I know best. But here's my take on the whole business.

Rolling was invented by the Inuit. Traditionally Inuit kayakers wore a sort of sealskin anorak, which was laced on to the cockpit rim, because there's no point in swimming: if you do, you're going to die. So, in order to survive they had to roll, and they practised a whole lot of different ways of doing it. Rolling with your paddle; rolling with your paddle behind your head; rolling with your paddle in the fingertips of one hand; rolling with your knife, harpoon, anything. And if you think a hand roll is a sweet move, try rolling with your hands tangled up in rope while being dragged through the water by an irate walrus that you've just harpooned.

⬆ **The forward finish position shared by the 'new school' rolls and the more traditional reverse screw roll.**

Many of these exercises were documented and brought to Europe by a missionary called Edi Hans Pawlata. He rolled using a technique we now call the Pawlata roll, namely that of gaining extra leverage by holding the paddle by the middle and one end. It's how many of us learnt to roll. But it's become kind of irrelevant, as have many of the other rolls you'll read about in old books, and hear about from old folks. Here's why.

The Inuit invented this technique in order to roll with their storm paddles. Inuit paddles were ridiculously skinny anyway, and on windy days they would take a special shorter paddle that was so dinky that they had to slide their hands from one end to the other just to paddle with it! This is called slide-hand technique, by the way, and is described in the Greenland-style section of the book. Anyway, no big surprise that they'd roll with this grip. But I think this method is completely redundant and silly when using a European-type paddle, unless you've no body language technique at all. Incidentally, in the dark times when I learnt to roll we were using 220cm (86in) paddles as well, so you needed a pretty big pool to practise in!

When you watch someone roll, you could be forgiven for thinking that they levered themselves upright with the paddle. But while this is just about possible, it isn't how skilful kayakers roll at all.

In fact, I'm going to go out on a limb and say that while there are many rolls that work very well on the principle of sweeping the blade through or across the water to generate lift, it's the body language that really matters. For instance, you can scull yourself upright using the old 'sculling for support' stroke, if you've mastered it – it's not something people do so much these days, but it's covered elsewhere in the book (see page 59). Equally, you can right yourself using body language alone, if you're good... or lucky... so surely, master a combination of the two skills and you should be pretty sorted.

Back when I first wrote about rolling, which was a horribly long time ago, boats were a different shape. Pool boats and whitewater boats were longer and narrower than they are now, and there wasn't much difference between the best way to roll boats like that, and the tried and tested Inuit techniques for rolling a sea kayak. And what I noticed over the intervening years is that as shortish boat designs evolved, my roll became more and more rubbish and scrappy.

The classic rolls, the screw roll and the reverse screw (which is sometimes called a back deck roll), are still a good way of righting a long, narrow and round-hulled boat, like a sea kayak, or a slalom-boat-derived design. But in very rough or shallow water, there's a popular roll which is more centred and less reliant upon the paddle sweep generating a lot of lift. It's also less likely to involve being dragged face down over rocks in shallow water. This roll has been called the storm roll, the put-across roll, the C-to-C roll, and probably many other things besides. My favourite name for it, coined by the late, great William Nealy, is the combat roll, and over the years I slowly stopped rolling in any other manner. It works in any boat, but it's particularly good in modern, short and wide whitewater and surf boats, for the following reasons:

■ It keeps you in the middle of the boat. These types of kayaks are very prone to rocking from end to end, so if you use a lot of front to back (or back to front) movement, especially combined with a sweeping action, you can roll up and find that you've made the boat 'ender', or stand on end. Which can be displeasing in the tricky situation which I assume you're probably in, or you wouldn't have fallen over in the first place!

■ It snaps the boat over very quickly and powerfully. The shape of these boats, especially the planing and semi-planing hull-design types, means that they're quite reluctant to roll on to and over their sidewall, and it takes a good snappy hip rotation to do it, rather than a slow progressive roll like the sweeping styles.

■ If you're in a hydraulic, or being pushed sideways by a broken wave, you don't want to be doing big exaggerated sweeps or lounging about on the back deck of the boat.

And of course, anything that gets you upright more quickly has to be a bonus, right?

The principle of the roll is that you bend to the side, arching your upper body up to the surface of the water on the side of the boat that you're going to roll, and place your paddle at 90° to the kayak. You then explosively bend your body the other way, down into the water, but since the paddle prevents it from moving downwards the result is that you're simply rotating your hips and righting the boat in one powerful snap.

Here are some ways to get that done. You'll ultimately need a boat that fits you properly (read the section on 'Outfitting', page 69) and with correctly adjusted footrests, a sprayskirt that seals it reasonably

↑ **The Pawlata grip, holding the paddle by one end for more leverage. Unnecessary unless everything else is wrong with your roll, or you are using a Greenland storm paddle!**

well and doesn't fall off when you twist and stretch, and a paddle. You may also benefit from swimming goggles and a noseclip, or a diving mask that covers both eyes and nose. This helps you to see what's going on, and keeps water from going up your nose. I'm pretty sure my sinuses have never been the same again since I learnt to roll without the benefit of these things.

LEARNING THE HIP ROTATION

If you're lucky, and/or a very kinaesthetic learner, you may have already grasped the concept of deliberate hip rotation while mastering some of the more basic skills in this book, but rolling tends to require taking it to the extreme. I struggled to learn it anyway.

When I learnt to roll it was from a book a little like this one. I was 12. I read the page about rolling over and over again, and I didn't really understand, but went out to try it anyway, all alone on a freezing November sea. Which I don't recommend, frankly. After a few attempts I was exhausted from swimming and emptying my boat. But I persevered, day after day, and you know what? I got absolutely nowhere.

↑ Practising the hip rotation in the kayak by holding on to the side of the pool.

The problem was that I didn't really understand the critical part. So much emphasis was placed on upper body motion, sweeping with the paddle in a specific way, throwing the head back flamboyantly at the end, that I didn't focus too much attention on the hips. The book mentioned something called a 'hip flick', but it didn't make a lot of sense to me, so I sort of glossed over it.

Shame really. Because the hip flick (or hip snap, as some like to call it) is *the only bit that matters!* The rest of the stuff we tell you to do is just overcomplicating the situation, giving you 17 things to think about so that your chances of doing them all at once are slim to anorexic. But almost no one gets the hip motion intuitively. So it does need to be backed up by a little bit of this and that.

Why do learners of the roll have trouble grasping it? I think it's because by the time we learn to kayak, we can already walk, run, jump, and in many cases do handstands and somersaults. In adulthood, we try to relate every new skill to a kinaesthetic experience we're already familiar with, and most people don't do anything in normal life that involves rotating one's hips from *side to side* by more than 90° in relation to one's torso. Yes folks. That's the move. That's all it is.

It's weird to practise it on dry land. It's hard to practise it anywhere. It's just a totally unnatural motion, until you can do it. Then it seems like the most natural thing in the world. I finally mastered it, about two years after my first abortive attempts, by standing in the doorway of the broom cupboard brandishing a yard brush instead of a paddle. But that's just my learning style. It needn't take two years. Half an hour would be more acceptable. So:

■ Draw, or find, a line on the ground.
■ Stand normally with your heels against the line.
■ Bend over by 90°. This is you sitting in a kayak. The line is the surface of the water. Stop thinking now.
■ Now, stand up for a moment, and turn around to stand facing the opposite way.
■ Put your toes against the line.

■ Bend over. Feel foolish yet? This is you sitting in the kayak *upside down*. The line is still the surface of the water. You are mostly underneath it. I said stop thinking.
■ Staying bent over, try to bend your head and torso around to one side as far as you can. I'm not especially bendy, but I can twist around until my head is somewhere over the line. That is analogous to being able to get your ear to the surface, just by bending to the side. Right, here comes the clincher.
■ Without moving your torso at all, jump a little and rotate your legs/feet by only 180° on the line. It's really easy.
■ Have a look at where you've ended up, and remind yourself that your upper body didn't move at all. It was kind of along the line (surface). It still is, or should be.
■ Do the little jump/rotate again. That's like rolling the other way, in your frame of reference. You can think now.
■ Keep practising. Get it dialled in. Try it as bent over as possible. But make sure the feet jump 180° each time.

Did you notice how we didn't talk about hips at all in that sequence? That's because moving your hips in that plane isn't a particularly normal thing to do or think about, whereas everyone knows how to move their head and feet.

Make sure you practise on both sides equally. Otherwise you can fall into the habit of learning to roll only one way, which, while better than nothing, will sooner or later let you down.

TAKING TO THE WATER

Now try this move you've learned on dry land, and try it in the kayak in some safe water. Leave your paddle and hold on to the side of a swimming pool, a low pontoon or jetty, or the bow of a friend's kayak. Lower your head into the water, and turn the boat as far upside down as you can with your legs, and then right it again using the little move we've practised. Leave your head in the water. It's important.

LEARNING THE BOW RESCUE

The bow rescue technique is a great stepping stone to being able to roll, but is also very useful as a recovery if you fail to roll or lose your paddle, and can save you and your friends from the hassle of a swim, emptying your boat and getting back in.

DOING THE ROLL WITH SOMEONE HELPING

The next stage is to add the paddle into the equation. Find somewhere the water is shallow enough for a helper to stand firmly about waist-deep. Capsize away from them with your paddle along the boat as shown. Keep your arms relaxed and allow your helper to wrap your back arm around the boat so that your hand is on the hull where the seat is, while holding the water blade in their other hand. When this position is in place, or they make a prearranged signal like banging on the boat, simply do your hip snap. Don't do anything else. Don't think about your arms or the paddle, just hold it and do the hip rotation. It'll work, I promise, but if for any reason it doesn't your helper can flip you upright or take your hands to right yourself as you did in the earlier drills.

Once you can do this, start to work on getting into position yourself, and just have the helper support the water blade with their hand. Ask them to notice whether your water blade is face down on the water when you roll, and if not, find out what you need to do with your wrists/arms to make sure that it is. Once you have that

⬆ **Bow rescue technique. You can hold your hands up like this and move them to and fro, until you feel the bow of your rescuer's kayak.**

⬆ **Using the bow rescue in a swimming pool. Grasp the front of the rescuer's boat with both hands and hip flick your own kayak upright.**

sorted out, you'll be rolling on your own, without any support from the helper. Yes, really...

Again, as soon as you're having some success, make sure you start to learn and practise on the other side. It's really worth being able to roll equally well on both sides and having no particular preference, for reasons I'll explain soon.

So, the combat roll is the roll I've always advocated, and in most cases taught to people first, without ever showing them the screw roll, reverse screw roll, etc. However, as time went on and the boats got even more extremely short and fat and funny looking, I started to rethink my roll a little bit, and it went like this.

It's pretty difficult to keep your paddle blade on the surface when the middle part of the boat is sooooo bulky. This often means that you finish the roll with a vertical paddle and the blade deep in the water, and that's not too good if it's shallow or you need support. I've often rolled up and immediately caught the end of the paddle on a rock and kind of lost it under the boat, resulting in an instant re-dunking or an

amusing (for the rest of the party) flailathon. Secondly, the sheer width of modern creek boats and playboats, and in many cases high seat position, mean that if your body language is any less than perfect, you can fail to roll, or at best finish in a kinda tenuous position.

So I've come up with this variant on the standard combat roll, and it goes something like this.

You bend your body to the side as per the normal C-to-C movement. That's why it's sometimes called a C-to-C roll, by the way, because you bend into a C shape one way, and then all the way across into a C shape the other. Anyway, the body movement is the same, but there's a little hint of sweeping the paddle too, as you would with the screw-type rolls. This helps to keep the paddle blade from sinking too deep. But we don't want to move the body towards the back of the boat, so at some point post hip snap we're gonna start sweeping the blade forwards again, just like sculling for support.

Of course, depending on where you find the paddle as you prepare to roll, you may find it better to start with a forward sweep and then back. And if the roll didn't go as well as planned, the good news is you keep sculling for support and you might not fall back in.

The other thing I like about the hybrid roll is that wherever the paddle is, you can just start sweeping it towards the mid-point 90° position and that'll generate lift immediately. Then you can hip snap the boat up when the paddle gets to the desired point. I've always done this, but actually it wasn't until I saw photos and video of it that I realised how much the boat is starting to roll upright as I sweep the paddle into position. The hip snap comes in quite late, when the paddle is perpendicular to the boat, and so has the maximum amount of leverage and hence support.

It's probably easier to learn this variation if you already have the forward and reverse screw rolls down, or if you're very good at sculling for support. My current thinking is that it's best to learn the combat C-to-C roll first, then the screw rolls or at least very good sculling, all in a boat that isn't too extremely short and fat, before merging all the skills together into this hybrid version.

So...

THE SCREW ROLL

Capsize in the same position as before, but this time tuck forward instead of to the side. Cock your wrist a little to make sure the leading edge of the water (front) blade is elevated, and start sweeping the paddle in a wide arc away from the boat. Try not to use your arms but your whole torso to move the paddle. Do the hip rotation thing smoothly as you sweep, and arch your head and body back as you finish. It's a super-powerful roll and should right you pretty effortlessly.

A tip: avoid pulling with your arms. This, and/or forgetting the hip rotation, are the usual things people fail on.

⬇ It's an awkward set-up position to practise the reverse screw roll, but in reality you'll find yourself in this very position underwater in many a wipe-out!

THE REVERSE SCREW ROLL

The reverse screw roll was invented because it's pretty common to find yourself lying flat on the back deck when you capsize, and wouldn't it be great to be able to roll from there instead of fight your way into position for another type of roll? Especially as you'll often find yourself with your paddle somewhere under you or behind your head.

For the purpose of clarity, I'm going to describe an anti-clockwise roll, or a down on the left and up on the right one, if you prefer.

Lie on the back deck. Put your right arm across your face as shown, keeping the paddle parallel to and close to the boat. Capsize to the left.

Now, wrap your left arm around the hull to put your hand 'under' the seat. This may feel familiar from the less convoluted rolls you've already learnt, but I'm not going to lie – everything else is probably feeling a bit weird right now!

Now sweep the right-hand blade out from the boat using your body, not your arms, and try to hip rotate the boat upright before the paddle gets to 90°. Keep your face and chest facing the bottom of the pool/river/ocean as far as possible.

You may have to cock your wrist the opposite way to what you learnt with the screw roll in order to keep the paddle on the surface. Otherwise, this weird-sounding roll is actually pretty foolproof apart from the total confusion you're likely to experience when you first try it. Once you trust it, however, it may well become your favourite roll.

ROLLING IN THE REAL WORLD

Unfortunately, when people take their newly learned rolling skills out into the wild, they usually find it difficult to apply what they learnt in a pool or at least a controlled environment. Water in the real world is cold and dark, you've capsized unexpectedly and can't seem to find the starting position that was so familiar in the learning stages. It's all taking too long, and you're starting to get flustered and panic for breath, so you give up and pull the sprayskirt.

The answer to this is probably twofold. Firstly, practise rolling all the time, if you can. Wherever you are, whatever the conditions, make sure you try out all your rolls on both sides. If it's cold, maybe when you get back from a trip or session, just before you get out and get warm. If the weather's OK, roll all the time, whenever you can.

Secondly, concentrate on your contact points. Head here, left hand and right hand there. If you have these and they're simple, they should be easy to find when you're underwater. Finally, practise holding your breath. But not 'take a deep breath' style – breathe out and practise having empty lungs, because it's this that panics people and makes them give up and bail out. So try to get used to it, if you can.

ROLLING IN DYNAMIC SITUATIONS

When you're in rough water, or even very windy conditions, you may be forced to roll on one side. The other side just won't work. On the other hand, rolling on the correct side will be extra super-easy. So it's important to have a rule of thumb for this problem. Here's how I approach the matter.

If you capsize, assume you're going to roll right through and up the other side, because 90% of the time that'll be right. Especially if you're quick. The thing that knocked or blew you over is probably going to be helping you up again in this scenario.

If you have to wait a bit, or the situation is extremely swirly (technical term), your boat may have changed position, and maybe it's not so certain which side to roll. So, if your roll doesn't finish successfully the first time, switch sides immediately and try the other.

These two strategies, between them, should get you back upright in almost every case. But, just for completeness, here's a bit more background on what conditions might be affecting the ease, or otherwise, of your rolls.

Steep waves

It's impossible to roll on the downwave side of a steep wave. If you're set up on that side in a wave train, wait until you're going down the back. How will you know? I think you'll feel it.

Hydraulics or surf

It's impossible to roll against the natural rotation of a breaking wave feature. Roll up on the wave side. In fact, don't even try – just reach out with your paddle into the face of the wave and it'll probably just lift you upright.

Whirlies

It's horrible trying to roll if your boat is being spun around by a whirlpool. The paddle always seems to get pulled down by the central vortex, or else the boat goes vertical as you roll up and you fall back in again. My strategy is to try once, and if it fails switch immediately to a reverse screw on the other side; and if that fails too, back to the first side. Whirlies are changing but fairly predictable features, and if one stroke is in the wrong place, another may well be OK as long as you're quick. Above all, don't give up, because whirlies don't last for long, and your very presence often collapses the vortex and lets you go.

Wind

In a strong wind it'll be easier to roll up on the windward side. Hang upside down for a second and you may actually feel which way the boat's trying to roll up – go with that.

ROLLING IN THE REAL WORLD

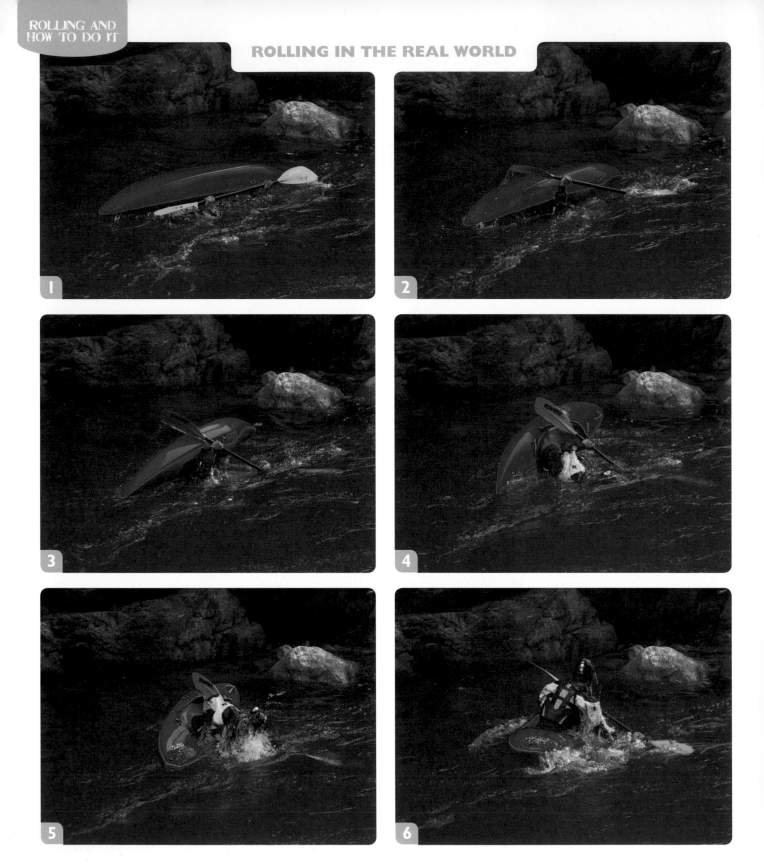

⬆ Rolling in the real world. The paddler has set up as for a screw roll, but makes a strong 'strike' at the water and follows it up with a hip action to right the boat. It's all over about halfway through the sequence and the rest of the recovery is from momentum and a little high brace support from the paddle.

↑ Reach out as far as you can from the side of the kayak with palms facing downwards, and hip flick the boat up while sweeping the arms down into the water.

↑ Many people prefer to finish the hand roll lying back for a low centre of gravity.

HAND ROLLING

Yes, it's possible, even quite easy, to roll without using a paddle. The role that hand rolling plays in the kayaker's repertoire is invaluable. Firstly, it gives a great deal of confidence to the paddler, and helps reduce that urge to cling on to the paddle for dear life. Which in turn improves the skill and subtlety of your paddling. Secondly, it's a genuinely useful skill on those rare occasions that you and your paddle are undergoing a temporary estrangement. And finally, it's a great way to make sure that your rolling body language is spot on and not over reliant on the paddle.

Having said that, I don't see as many people hand rolling as I used to. The main reason for that is that many types of boat are quite difficult to roll these days. Polo boats, slalom boats, sea kayaks and the like are still relatively low and narrow, and can be hand rolled with ease, but the shorter, fatter whitewater boats that are currently in vogue are a bit harder, as I've discussed in the previous section.

However, I'd still recommend having a go at hand rolling, and here are the two ways that I've found work for most people.

Front deck hand roll

This is really a C-to-C/combat/storm roll body movement, but because you have no support from the paddle to finish, it's important to keep the centre of gravity as low as possible at the end, and this is achieved by pressing your chest on to the front deck as you complete the roll.

Adopt the C-to-C starting position, but instead of wrapping an arm around the boat, reach straight up into the air with them. Then bring your arms down on to the water, keeping them straight, and if possible turn them so your palms are downwards. I find it helps to turn my head to look down, and then the arms can be in the right orientation without undue contortions. Push your hands out away from the boat as much as possible.

Now, at this point many people smash their palms downwards into the water to achieve the support they need during the hip rotation phase. Me, I prefer to do a sort of doggy paddle-type action, one hand at a time. It might be less of a powerful impulse but with two or three strokes (say left-right-left) I can keep the support going for longer and do a slower, smoother hip flick.

Back deck hand roll

I like the back deck hand roll in lower-volume boats, or ones with low back decks anyway. It doesn't seem to work well in creek boats.

You can either start from the same C-to-C position and then throw your weight backwards instead of forwards, or you can start from lying on the back deck. Either way, you're only going to be able to keep one arm in play after the initial strike. After that you're going to be lying on your back and swiping downwards with what we might term the water hand, or the hand that would have been holding the water blade if you had a paddle. The best thing to do with the other arm is fling it across to the other side of the boat as a sort of balance weight. It can't do much, but every little helps in this rather tenuous finishing position!

Having said that hand rolling is a useful exercise and an occasionally more than helpful skill, I'd like to qualify that with one further comment, which is this. Some people become very good at hand rolling and just can't be bothered with the paddle. Rather than battle to get the paddle into the right position to roll, they just drop it and hand roll, expecting to pick up the paddle once they're upright. This is a really bad habit, as in any conditions where you might really capsize by accident it's likely that the paddle might be carried away from you, leaving you vulnerable – or at best a nuisance to your friends.

↓ The leaning forward finish allows you to keep your weight low too, and is possibly a safer and more stable recovery.

MORE LAUNCHING

It may seem a bit strange to come back to it now, since I've already explained the basics of putting your kayak in the water, but sometimes you need to launch somewhere a bit inconvenient, and the skills and strokes we've just covered are kind of the minimum qualification for some of these situations. So now that you can do balancing strokes and roll and stuff, it might be worth looking at this again.

BEACH LAUNCH

The best way to launch from a shallow sloping beach, if there are any waves at all, is to place the boat facing directly into the water. Put the sprayskirt on, and then use a hand on one side and a paddle on the other to push the kayak out into the waves, concentrating on keeping the boat straight. If you try to get in the boat while it's floating, it will be too difficult. And it'll almost certainly get turned sideways, and washed back on to the beach.

SURF LAUNCH

Surf kayaks usually have fins on them. You can beach launch them in the usual way, but you really have to lift yourself up to move the fins in the sand until you're in deep enough water to paddle away. These boats are generally too fragile to seal launch from anything but a sandy beach, unless you have the luxury of a boat to ferry you to the waves!

SEAL LAUNCH

The seal launch is the usual way to get into fast flowing water. It just isn't practical to get in and fit your sprayskirt while the kayak is afloat. Take a look at the way the current is moving, and make sure that when you hit the water you'll be poised and ready for what's coming up. If you seal launch from a great height, it's not unlike running a waterfall. You need to think about your entry angle, and accept that you may not get the landing you wanted. Don't land flat in green water from more than a metre or two in height (3–6ft). It hurts.

→ **This photo conveys some of the potential problems of seal launching: sharp, angular rocks and a large drop into surging water. The paddler needs to land when the water surges up to cover the rocks at the bottom. If he capsizes he'll be dragged upside down over barnacle-covered rock. Lovely...**

OUTFITTING

If you paddle any closed-cockpit kayak, then a bit of outfitting is required to make the boat fit your physical form perfectly, and this can make more difference to your performance than you might imagine. Firstly, a comfortable paddler is a happy and skilful one. You aren't going to be much good in your kayak, or have a fun day, if your legs are going to sleep and your hips and knees are bruised and battered. Secondly, if the boat fits you like a glove, it will react instantaneously to your slightest movement, and just as importantly you'll instantly feel any force that the water applies to the hull. Which helps, believe me.

Back in the day, outfitting a boat was a bit of a black art, requiring tools and materials that not everyone had to hand. I don't mean eye of newt and toe of frog, but it was gonna take more than household items, and there were a lot of mistakes to be made.

Nowadays, whitewater kayaks in particular come with extensive outfitting kits included, with pre-moulded bolt-in and strap-on components designed for Generation X-Box. But you still need to do a bit of work, if you're going to have an awesome set-up. Incidentally, although I've used whitewater boats for the photos here, everything I'm about to say is equally applicable to sea kayaks, surf kayaks, polo boats, anything. I can't think of any kind of canoe or kayak that wouldn't benefit from comfortable, positive points of contact for the paddler.

Unfortunately, most people make a lazy or just downright incompetent job of outfitting their boat. Some just can't get their head around investing a whole day in getting the boat ready to paddle – and it is very time-consuming, sitting in the boat trying bits of foam, testing, trimming, checking again. Some folks, perhaps, don't realise how much additional sensitivity, power transmission and paddling performance (or a steeper learning curve) they can attain from having a super-well-fitting boat. As a friend of mine used to say with a wink, every time he saw a dodgy roll or a less than confident support stroke, 'Nice hip pads...'.

So, if I've convinced you to spend a day of your life (probably) with your head in your boat, what you are going to need is mostly shown in the photo on the right. It's not always easy to buy blocks of the type of closed cell ether-foam and self-adhesive mat that the pros use, and it's expensive stuff, so I hoard every piece I come across. If you just can't get it or afford it, you can make thick foam by gluing together layers of Karrimat or similar proprietary closed cell polyethylene foam sleeping/ yoga mats. What a mouthful. Camping mats. You know what I'm on about. The cheaper the better. The important thing is that the foam is quite dense and firm.

If you do want to source it yourself, the optimum for polyethylene closed cell seems to be 30 to 33kg/m³. It's the same density that is used for most impact-protection applications. We're not upholstering a sofa here – we need padding that transmits your body language to the boat instantly, not some time next week. The fit we're looking for is zero pressure, but zero movement as well. This is worth investing a lot of time in.

Here comes the obligatory science lesson. Most of the padding in your boat is going to be held in place with some sort of adhesive. Adhesive – glue, if you like – is very, very strong and resistant to sheer (which in this case means force perpendicular to the direction of the

⬆ **Outfitting your boat is a serious business, and you're going to need a few things...**

bond), and often very weak when subjected to peeling force. Think of a sticker. Easy to peel off from one corner, almost impossible to shift by pushing it sideways. That's the end of the science bit, I promise, but remember this as you work.

The first thing to do is check that the boat is dry and free from spiders, both very important things. Glue won't stick in the wet, and spiders are horrible. Doubly so if they get in your glue. This is always something that I have a massive OCD about, because how is the boat going to dry with the cockpit cover on and, if it's not on, clearly it's going to fill up with spiders! I'm going to leave you to deal with that whole issue on your own, because it's just too traumatic and I need to finish this. Suffice to say, outfit your boat when it's brand new and don't let it get wet or full of spiders.

If you need to use glue (see the photos above), follow the instructions and allow the proper amount of time for each stage! This may be more or less time than estimated on the packaging, depending on temperature and humidity. I like to use waterproof PVA (it must be the waterproof sort) because I'm done sticking my head in a boat full of solvent fumes, but you can use Evo-Stik or any wetsuit adhesive if you like that sort of thing. If you don't have a workshop table, I recommend doing the gluing on your actual boat, as I have here. It's easy to clean excess glue off shiny boats, not so much off your coffee table. However, be careful if you clean your boat with solvents like white spirit, because it can smear the decals/graphics off, which is a bit upsetting.

⬇ **Duct tape isn't used to hold foam in place (with one exception in my boats – see text), but it can be handy to protect any exposed edges from peeling as you get into the boat. This photo also shows how I used hosepipe to make handles for removable foam blocks. This one is the 'suicide block' in my squirt boat.**

If your boat comes with ready-moulded hip pads and back strap, as shown in the photo here, then you'll only have to adjust these to give you a tight but comfortable fit. On the hips this is done by inserting some rigid foam behind the pads. It can be the self-adhesive type, or a block of closed cell foam or several layers of camping mat glued together. Whatever you can get. The important thing is that you can slide in and out, but once in, there should be no room to wiggle whatsoever. If you're starting from nothing you should try to make a shape out of foam like the ones the manufacturers supply. This will mean a wedge shape, thinner at the bottom than the top, and with a pronounced bulge at the top front corner to wrap around the front of your hips. It can take a while to carve this with a knife and/or surform, but you'll end up with a perfect fit eventually. Or you can just buy one. The ready-made ones are pretty good.

If you don't have a back strap, I definitely recommend buying one. It's possible to make a back support by shaping a large block of foam, as shown in the photo, or to make your own out of webbing, but it's very difficult to make something as comfortable and safe as a commercially available back strap.

Once you have the hips and back strap sorted, try to make sure that you cannot lift your backside off the seat. Clearly, you need to be able to get out by sliding back or whatever, but if you're upside down you don't want to hang off the seat. If you have too much play in this area, it's back to the drawing board.

In the knee area, it's less common to find ready-prepared padding. Usually all that's required, though, is a thin layer of foam to add a little comfort and grip, and this can be achieved with the thin self-adhesive

foam supplied, or with glue and cheap camping mat.

They say that clothes make the man. I don't know about that, but they definitely make a huge difference to your fit in the boat. The first thing to do is to get into the boat wearing the actual kit that you wear when paddling. If that varies, choose the bulkiest. Don't think that your jeans and trainers are going to be a close enough approximation, or you'll be slopping around in that boat like a complete novice. It's best

⬆ **Yes, if that's what you wear in the boat.**　⬆ **Wrong. Any way.**

to do all this with no one else around, because you'll be at the mercy of the sort of comedians who like to draw attention to the fact that you're dressed as a gimp in your driveway. Or share hilarious and original (not) jokes about Noah and/or 'Expecting a flood?' because you're sitting in a boat nowhere near any water. Boat outfitting is best done in private, therefore, so that you aren't tempted to chase these comic geniuses up the road with the bread knife.

Now that you're in, slide a bit of foam under the knee/thigh grip area, and work out what you need. It's a great idea to draw around it

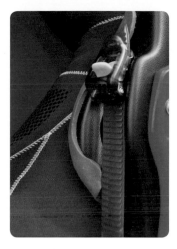

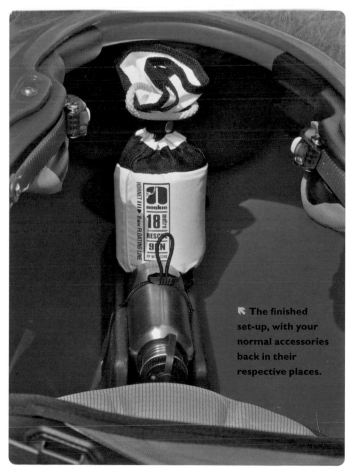

with a marker pen, but don't cut out the exact shape! Cut it oversized, so that you have an extra bit to wrap around the edges.

Once you've got the piece in place, trim off the corners as per the photo – think how easy it is to peel things from the corners. We don't want that.

Finally, stick the excess up and around the plastic/fibreglass so that there are no edges exposed that would scuff and peel back as you wriggle into the boat, as shown here.

Now it's time to take a look at the feet. If you have a plate-style footrest, it could do with some padding, which is usually supplied with new boats. Depending on the length of your legs and the resulting footrest position, you may need to trim this to size. Try not to have any space around the foam. If it's tight against the hull and deck you're less

likely to be injured or wrong-footed by slipping your toes in the gap. So give this the time it deserves. Sometimes it's worth dismantling the footrest altogether and using the plate as a template or guide.

I like to pad the footrest rails on plate footrests or any other type, because they seem to be a very good way of injuring your feet. However, they attack foam as much as they do toes, and so does the process of getting your feet into the boat, so I simply wrap some padding round them with duct tape instead of gluing anything in place. This protects the foam and makes it easy to replace when you trash it.

My final piece of protection is for my heels. You may not feel that you need this if you always wear very sturdy shoes in your boat, but if you use socks or wetsuit boots it adds a lot of comfort and luxury. I cut a round piece of foam mat, because a rounded shape is the most resistant to peeling and damage, and stick it to the inside of the hull where my heels rest.

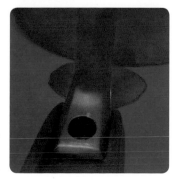

If you need to make any

components removable to facilitate getting in or out of the boat, I recommend using a piece of hosepipe with a rope through it to make a handle, and another piece to reinforce the foam and stop your rope from cutting into or through it. It's easy to punch a hole in the foam with a big screwdriver and force a piece of hose through. It looks smart and is safe and effective. I like to use washing machine hose, rather than the garden variety, because it's tougher, and it's red as opposed to camouflaged, which isn't always what you want for a safety handle.

Now reinstall all the gear that you habitually carry, and make sure that access and comfort are all that you'd hope for. You won't know finally whether there's a dodgy bit that makes your leg go to sleep until you've been in the boat for hours at a time, but safety is paramount from the outset. Make sure you fill all the spare space in front of and behind the cockpit area with airbags, inflate them properly and tie them in. This makes a huge difference to the safety, rigidity and durability of your boat... it's so important.

Finally, take a look at your handiwork, and think about the whole sheer/peel science that I mentioned at the beginning. Get in and out of the boat a few times, and if there are any bits that look vulnerable at the edges, consider using duct tape to protect them.

Finished? OK, whack a cockpit cover on your boat to keep it dry while everything cures, and more importantly to keep spiders out of the cockpit. I hate spiders. Gross.

↘ **The finished set-up, with your normal accessories back in their respective places.**

CHAPTER 3

OPEN WATER

When you take your kayak further away from the shore than you can swim, you may need to know a little more than just how to paddle, steer and stop. This section, then, is for you. And it has many nice pictures in it...

A KAYAK IS NOT LIKE A CAR

Readers who've grown up playing with boats will already be aware that there's a difference between boats and, for instance, cars, or bicycles, or skateboards. Boats don't stay still. And boats don't respond to your movements the way you think they're going to if you've always spent your time on dry land. It's not a bad thing, just a different thing. So here are three pieces of advice:

◻ Your boat won't just stay where you left it. Keeping it in one place, unless you tie it to something, is exhausting and frustrating. So my advice is, don't try.
◻ Don't think about your motion relative to the ground. You're in the water and the air: these are the things to think about.
◻ Don't think that your safety hangs on slamming on the brakes every time you're unsure of yourself. You're not riding a bicycle. In fact, in most situations speed is your friend.

Now that you can paddle your kayak around pretty well, I need to explain some basic rules and etiquette before we go too much further.

A kayak is a pretty small thing compared to a lot of water craft and you might be forgiven for thinking it doesn't really matter where you go and what you do. And very often it doesn't. But other people use the water too, and it's good to know what they consider to be the rules of the road. Or river. Or sea. Or whatever.

The first thing to know is, who has right of way? The general pecking order is that powered craft have to give way to everyone else and allow them to continue with their chosen speed and path. Rowed or paddled boats are next – we have to give way to sailors under all circumstances. And everyone should give way to swimmers. The exception to this is when a powered craft is in a 'restricted navigation'. This means where the water is too shallow or too narrow for them to change direction or stop in control. Larger boats/ships will play this card every time. Don't paddle out in front of a ship and expect them to stop or go around you. It isn't going to happen. In fact they probably won't even see you!

The next thing on the agenda is, drive on the right. If it's a river or a narrow channel of any kind, the rule is to leave oncoming traffic to your left, or overtake people going the same way as you so that they're on your right-hand side. Usually this really doesn't matter in a kayak or any small boat, but it's just as well to understand that that is the rule so that what everyone is doing makes sense!

A lot of places have speed limits, though you're unlikely to break them in a kayak. But one of the side effects of a speed limit is that people who drive fast boats often drive them at just the right speed to make a massive wake or wash that can swamp you. Honestly, I often wish they had just gone past at full speed, because the wave might have been much smaller. But look out for this, and especially if the driver sees you and slows down just in time to make the wave he throws at you as big as humanly possible!

When you first take up kayaking, falling in the water is often a worry. For some people that concern never goes away. But you don't have to get wet to enjoy paddling. Using the techniques outlined in this book, and a bit of forethought about where to go, plus a modicum of common sense, it's perfectly possible to take your kayak out and enjoy it without ever setting foot, or worse still head, in the water. And that's perfect for a lot of people.

A stable kayak like a sit-on, an inflatable or an open-cockpit touring or family boat is the obvious choice. It's not the only choice, however, since you can quickly acquire the skills to paddle a faster touring boat, or a fitness kayak or racing K-boat, without much risk of falling in. But whether you're a beginner on a sit-on, or a hard-charging K-boat racehead, it's pretty important that you choose a paddling venue that's not going to challenge you with waves or currents or anything else that you or your choice of boat can't handle.

Lakes or sheltered lagoons are a good choice, or large slow-moving rivers or estuaries that aren't prone to currents or tides. Unexpected weirs are bad news too. But put just a little thought into where you go, and what boat you're paddling, and you should be able to have fun without an unwelcome dunking.

↓ A stable touring kayak is an excellent choice for flat water paddling, combining reasonable speed with a good degree of stability.

→ Once you are confident, it's equally possible to paddle a sea boat or other fast kayak without fear of getting wet.

TOURING

If you're going to cover a bit more ground, venture into the unknown, or paddle when conditions may be changeable (wind, waves, tides and currents) you might prefer to paddle a boat that goes through the water a bit better and has a few features to make life easier on a journey. Although there are large-cockpit touring boats for those who don't want to address capsizing or really dynamic paddling, the boats that do the job best are longer, narrower, enclosed touring kayaks. Space for different clothes and equipment, decklines and shockcords for basic essentials, and a more 'seaworthy' type of hull are the things that make this sort of paddling into accessible fun. But now that we're venturing more into the unknown, it's a good idea to make sure that capsizing, getting in and out of the kayak and basic boat-to-boat rescue skills are in place in case the conditions do get the better of you when you're far from help.

⬇ **With safety in numbers, it's exciting to venture further afield and onto stretches of water that take you further from shore.**

➔ **High spec touring kayaks can take you anywhere you want to go, and can carry food and camping equipment for multi-day trips.**

TRIPPING OR CAMPING WITH YOUR KAYAK

A lot of people enjoy going on a multi-day adventure in their boats, and kayaking and camping seem to go well together. The key is to travel light. Another key is to keep everything dry!

You can use any type of kayak for overnight trips, from a sit-on to a full-bore sea kayak. The sea kayak is going to be the more organised, since the different hatches and compartments make life a lot easier, but carrying a sea boat full of gear is no fun at all, and there are other ways of keeping your gear dry even if it's outside the boat.

The roll-top dry bag is a staple piece of equipment for many kayakers. Simply put in your gear, roll the top down three times and close the buckle, and whatever is inside will stay dry even if you dunk the whole bag underwater. You can get them in many shapes and sizes – personally I find that separating different types of gear by using several small bags is much better than having one or two larger ones. If I put all my gear in one place, it trends towards the wettest common denominator as time goes on! I like bags that have rucksack straps on them, to make it easier to move them to and from the kayak. The other thing that's super-useful is to have some sort of tie-down loops on the bag so you can lash it in place.

Some people like to use screw-top plastic containers instead of small drybags. They aren't really any heavier, and have the advantage of being rigid, which may be good for more fragile items. Although I'm struggling to think of a fragile item I might want to take kayaking. But it always seems right to me to keep food in a rigid container.

It's very easy not to take enough water with you on a kayaking adventure. Maybe it's not an issue, if you're paddling in clean, fresh water, or simply passing lots of civilisation along the way. But otherwise, think about it. Water is heavy, so some way of boiling or purifying river water could be a good option.

Even if you take a tent with you, it's also pretty useful to have some sort of tarpaulin or 'tarp' to use as a groundsheet or a canopy.

← A roll-top dry bag offers ample water-tight storage space.

↓ Waterproof plastic containers are a good alternative for fragile items. These chemical containers are a pretty popular choice and come in lots of sizes.

I like to take a hammock and a tarp, and a bivvy bag in case of really bad conditions. I hate tents – they're heavy, a hassle to put up and take down, and always seem to be wet and full of other people's disorganised kit. But maybe that's just me...

A throwline or towline and paddles can be used to make a washing line, or to string up your tarp. In fact everything should have a dual purpose, in the interest of travelling light. The climbing slings and karabiners that are so useful for many kayaking situations will also prove invaluable when tying down or hanging up your makeshift camp.

FREYA HOFFMEISTER

Freya Hoffmeister, the 'Woman in Black', is based in Husum, North Germany, when she's not travelling or sea kayaking around the world. Then she chooses her van, a tent or a rental car to sleep in. Independence is her lifestyle.

She is accomplished in several styles of paddling, including open-water marathon racing, Greenland-style rolling, huge expeditions and rough-water kayaking – and who knows what else she's going to try next?

Freya chooses boats, paddles and gear depending on conditions, her mood, and pure chance. A squeeze into a squirt boat, a sidestep to whitewater rivers, a sprint and balance act on a surf ski, it's all about variety in life! No time for her to get bored, and when you see her having fun playing around, or experience her endurance on a race or trip, you'll start to feel what a kayaker's life is all about.

Her latest huge trip took her right around Australia. She was 332 days under way, solo and mostly unsupported. It's considered to be THE challenge for a sea kayaker, and had only been finished once before – 27 years earlier. For news of her latest challenges, visit freyahoffmeister.com.

In a previous section I talked about some ways to transport your kayak, by hand, on a trolley, or on the roof of a car or van. But when you decide to travel abroad with a boat, there are a whole lot of other things to think about.

My first piece of advice is, don't. If you can rent or borrow a kayak at your destination, or at least in the right country, it will save a fair amount of bother. But if you must make your kayak your travelling companion, here are some tips and handy tricks.

Smaller kayaks like modern creek and playboats (anything under 3m/10ft really) aren't too much hassle at airports. You can usually rock up with your kayak and check in without any questions being asked. Some people like to put it in a bag, and say it's a surfboard bag. But generally there's no problem, you just have to take it to a special oversized luggage area, because it won't fit on the suitcase conveyor belt.

Some airlines do have a length limit. You may want to check before booking and avoid them. Most, however, have a category for 'One piece of sporting equipment' that flies free or for a fixed fee, and no length limit. Read the baggage policy of the airline properly and work out whether you want to put all your luggage inside the kayak, or keep the kayak light and check in additional bags. It's all about the baggage allowance and the excess baggage charges.

Some check-in personnel are more clued up than others. The fact is a 3m kayak will fit in the hold of a plane. It's just like two or three suitcases, and carried by one man. So it's not impossible or even difficult. But sometimes it's just easier for them to say 'No'.

If your kayak is a longer one, you're going to struggle. Always consult with the airline first. They'll probably give you an airfreight quote for flying it.

In all cases, have a plan B. There's no point getting your kayak refused if you need it for your adventure or competition. But the problem is, most airlines will refuse kayaks or quote an astronomical price if you phone to enquire in advance. So my fallback would be, get a quote for airfreight before you plan the trip. If you're OK with it, take someone to the airport with you who can, if your kayak doesn't get on the plane with you, drive it to the freight terminal and ship it to your destination.

The miracle solution to kayak travel trauma is the folding or inflatable kayak. This will check-in at the airport or train station without any raised eyebrows, you can carry it on your back, and whatever your onward travel plans, it's unlikely to be a problem.

←↑ **Most of your travel problems evaporate if you can find a pack-down kayak that suits your paddling needs.**

→ **Think outside the box. This bike carriage on a Swiss train welcomes kayakers, and we actually used it to run the shuttle.**

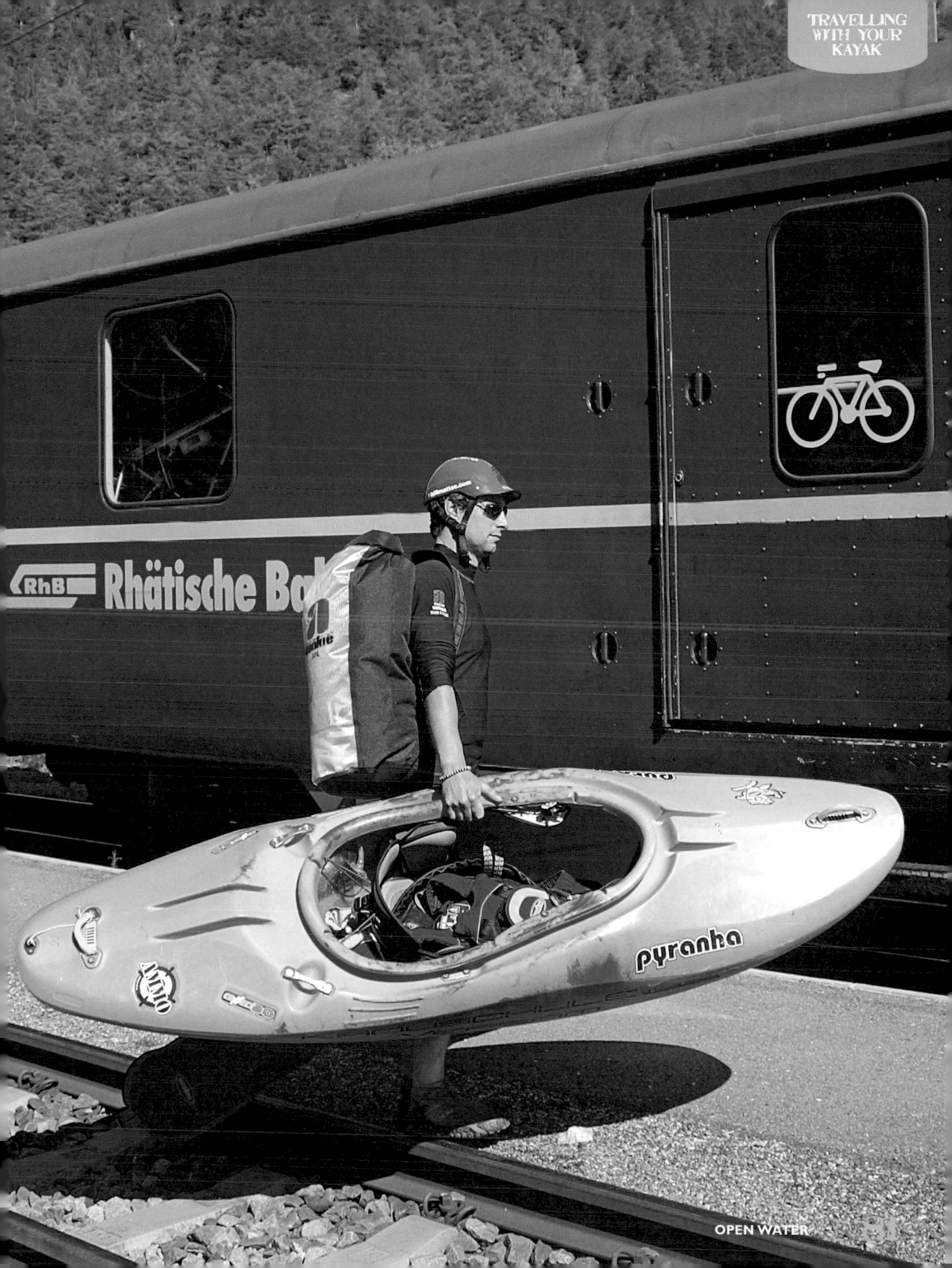
RhB Rhätische Ba
pyranha

SAFETY, RESCUE AND RECOVERY

While good planning and appropriate equipment can and will prevent many difficulties, accidents still happen. This section is intended to make you aware of some of the issues, so that you'll always be prepared. More detailed advice on the correct equipment is found in other sections of this book, but you should be aware at all times that while the right gear is an important contributing factor to safety in any situation, the right mindset is even more so.

Practise the following techniques to a proficient level, and make sure that you know how to use any equipment at your disposal. Otherwise it'll just waste your time and get in the way when every second counts and you need to get it right.

COMMUNICATION

The biggest part of safety and rescue on the water is communication. Make sure you're realistic about your own level of ability and experience and that of your paddling group. Keep a regular dialogue going as much as is possible, so that everyone is aware of each other. If something goes wrong, keep communicating. This is important to enable the most experienced/able paddler on hand to take the right action, and to reassure the victim. People start to feel isolated and scared very quickly when something is wrong and no one is talking to them.

CAPSIZE DRILL

How to do it is covered in detail on page 39. Everyone going canoeing or kayaking should be confident that they're capable of competently exiting the boat in the event of a total capsize. If you don't think someone is safe to do this, you should say something. It's fairly common to capsize even in calm water,

and whether someone can get out of the boat when it happens isn't really something that should be left to chance!

BOAT-TO-BOAT RESCUES

It's often possible to swim or wade to safety after a capsize, with no harm done. If, however, you're in deep water or far from shore, it's handy to have practised some boat-to-boat rescue techniques. With the exception of sit-on-tops, which you can right and climb straight back on board, most kayaks will need to be emptied before you can get back in.

The best way to empty a kayak is to lift it up on its side so that most of the water comes out as you do so, and then rock it to and fro upside down to drain out any water that's left. This can be done by one person holding each end, whether on land or in kayaks, or across the deck of another kayak while afloat, or simply over one person's knee as shown here.

If you're swimming following a capsize your kayak can be placed alongside another and steadied by hand while you climb back on top. It's a bit fiddly, but with this extra bit of stability most people can get back on board, and then re-enter the cockpit just as if they were on dry land.

TOWING

Sometimes, whether because of injury, tiredness, or broken equipment, it's necessary to undertake towing another paddler or their boat. You can use a variety of different methods, whether boat-to-boat, or using a specialist waist towline, or just a webbing sling over your arm or shoulder.

The most important consideration is to ensure that in the event of a capsize, neither the tower nor the towee is putting themselves in more danger than they were in before the rescue was undertaken. For more info about towing, see pages 120 and 152.

1

2

SEA KAYAKING

It's with not a little trepidation that I broach the subject of sea kayaking, because grammatically speaking it's a minefield. It could mean paddling in the sea, with a sit-on kayak, a ski or a surf kayak. Or does it mean 'using a sea kayak', generally accepted to mean an Inuit-style boat? That's awkward too, because you could paddle a sea kayak on a lake or a river. Would that still be sea kayaking? I've baffled myself! Well, I'm going to proceed thus: in my parlance, paddling on the sea but staying close to the shore, while surfing or sunning yourself on the sit-on top, is not sea kayaking. Venturing out into deeper water and more than swimming distance from the shore, however, is a different kettle of fish. To paddle on open water like a big lake, or a wide river, or on the sea, it makes sense to use a fast kayak that tracks well and can handle rough water, should the need arise. That's either going to mean a sea kayak, or something broadly similar to one that's been developed for inland use. So if I randomly chop and change between referring to 'sea kayaks' and 'open water' paddling, I hope that you'll forgive me and try to keep up.

Sea kayaking (by which I mean paddling a sea kayak, not merely paddling any old kayak on the sea) has a special place in my heart, since it's what's known as an aboriginal form of the sport. This is nothing

↑ The author with a Greenland-style paddle and a contemporary traditional sea kayak.

to do with aboriginal Australians, although they too have a place in paddling history which I may one day explore. No, by aboriginal I mean existing from the earliest of times, and in the case of sea kayaking it was the Inuit indigenous to Arctic and sub-Arctic regions who were aboriginal. They made slender kayaks from skins and bones, and paddled them in horrifying seas and sub-zero temperatures using woefully inadequate driftwood paddles and the questionable practice of stitching one's coat to the cockpit rim to stop the water getting in. All of which is of historical interest, but the astonishing thing is this: our best attempt at seagoing kayaks today look just like the ones the Inuit used. Materials have improved. Paddles and sprayskirts make a bit more sense too. But the Inuit chaps spent thousands of years kayaking, and unsurprisingly we can't seem to improve much on their ideas.

Mind you, they were a single-minded folk. In their own language the word Inuit means 'the real people'. They knew when they were right, because when they weren't they were dead. The Arctic isn't a forgiving place to live off the land (or sea), even now. Here's a little anecdote:

Here I am paddling a boat that has a rudder, but one that can be flipped up out of the water by pulling a cord when not in use. Which seems to me the best of both worlds.

INUIT STUFF

Here's a bit of nonsense for you:

- The Inuit used to commit suicide if they became old enough or ill enough to eat more than they could provide.
- They were condemned by the French for eating nothing but meat, yet were the most eco-sensitive race imaginable, keeping their own survival and nature in a delicate balance.
- They were nearly wiped out economically by the Europeans, because their bartering system revolved around how much they needed, not how much they could get.

During the 19th century, an Inuk (singular of Inuit) was out fishing and became separated from his buddies in a storm, somewhere off the coast of Greenland. He landed, rather cross, in Scotland, about 1,000 miles away. Not, I imagine, knowing where Scotland was. Is, even. After a bite to eat with the locals, he was all for lacing himself back into his kayak and setting off for home, but was persuaded or

forcibly prevented from leaving by his Victorian hosts, who probably thought that his crazy little boat wouldn't make it to the nearest island, let alone Mars where he clearly came from. So he stayed, and made a bit of an effort to integrate into Scottish society, but pretty soon he became depressed and died.

I tell you all this because (a) I'm sure it's where Spielberg got the idea for ET, (b) I think it's amazing (and it's true, recorded in the parish records of some obscure town I've forgotten the name of), and (c) because all this history is a big part of the character of the sea kayak. It's a good feeling when I realise why they're the way they are today, and to understand what the boat is capable of even if we are not. I now see why some people paddle with unnecessarily ineffectual traditional Greenland paddles. It connects us with their admirable inventors.

OK, back to sea kayaking. Sea boats are very traditional-looking but often have modern design features like drop-down skegs for excellent tracking, decklines, a large keyhole cockpit and plastic or composite construction. They have sealed compartments with large waterproof hatches, and so can be filled with the necessities of your expedition without fear of damp equipment at your journey's end.

This means that we can get comfortable using the adjustable back strap and footrests, put on the spraydeck, and then push ourselves into the water. For paddling in rough conditions you need to fit tightly in the boat, but a pedal footrest design allows you to slide your feet off the pedals and straighten the legs for comfort when you don't need to be braced in. Neat. The keyhole cockpit is now the norm, and takes the same spraydeck as most modern boats, which is very handy.

TO RUDDER, OR NOT TO RUDDER?

There's a great deal of controversy and disagreement about the need or otherwise for a rudder on a sea kayak. Usually I'm down for a bit of controversy, but in this case I don't really know what all the fuss is about. I think if you're a skilful kayaker, you'll be able to control and direct a sea kayak very easily without the need for a rudder, especially if you have a drop-down skeg. And rudder mechanisms do tend to be excessively complex, and need a lot of maintenance and attention to stop them seizing up or filling with sand. But if you're a predominantly placid water paddler and you prefer to use a rudder than to lean the boat over, then why not? I've paddled boats with or without rudders and I can't bring myself to feel strongly one way or the other.

Sea kayaks are fairly stable, with the exception of a couple of really extreme designs, but they don't need to be too stable. If you paddle a wide, flat-bottomed boat on the sea it is constantly tipping and wriggling, as it tries to stay flat to the water no matter what angle the water has decided to adopt. The sea kayak allows you to stay upright no matter what, but is stable enough that you don't need to keep moving or support yourself with the paddle.

The sea kayak is a surprisingly manageable beast. OK, it doesn't exactly turn on a sixpence, but it's manoeuvrable enough once you've learnt the trick of tipping it dramatically to release the keeled part from the water. Small adjustments to direction are simple enough even without a rudder, and a drop-down skeg enhances tracking if the wind will persist in blowing you off course.

Rolling is easier in a sea kayak than it is in most boats, and can work quite a lot better if you use an old-school screw roll rather than the aggressive modern variants practised by playboaters. The boat also has an enormous amount of final stability when on its side, which means that if your sculling for support (an art lost to the younger boating generation, I fear) is up to scratch, you may never need to roll at all!

A sea kayak is a many splendoured thing. Whether in waves or calm water, the boat acquits itself with all the decorum one could hope for, and is a genuinely practical way to enjoy the ocean. It gets us to places other craft couldn't manage, and allows an experienced paddler to be entirely self-sufficient on the open sea. The Inuit hunter would be proud of you.

TRADITIONAL SEA KAYAKING

Aficionados of traditional sea kayaking, more commonly known as Greenland kayaking, like to follow as closely as possible the techniques and equipment styles of the Inuit people from whose aboriginal and prehistoric roots we get the concept of the kayak as we know it today. But although most people call it Greenland style, this really refers to a culture that spans a wide Arctic area from Siberia to Greenland, and there are also many influences from Aleutian cultures, which also reach from Russia to North America but are primarily sub-Arctic.

Enough with the history lesson. The main thing about traditional kayaking is that enthusiasts try to use kayaks, paddles and in some cases clothing that emulate as closely as is practical the kind of thing that the Inuit or Aleut islanders would have done. These may be made 'traditionally' or be replicas made using modern technology, but aside from the materials, in most cases what the original kayakers developed over thousands of years is still pretty hard to improve upon.

Most sea kayaks actually look very reminiscent of traditional Inuit or Aleutian boats, but they tend to be made with rounded hulls, which were very difficult to achieve in a skin on frame construction, but are actually stiffer and more durable when using modern plastics. However, the 'Greenland' boater prefers the chined hull design, even in a composite kayak.

HOWARD JEFFS

Howard Jeffs has been sea kayaking for over 42 years, and in 1983 became the youngest BCU Level 5 sea coach of the time. The following year he achieved the same position with the Mountaineering Instructors Certificate. Although very fortunate to have worked and paddled in waters around most of Europe, Arctic Norway, Svalbard and Greenland, North America, Sri Lanka, the Maldives and the Galapagos Islands, his love for the diverse west coast of Britain remains ever strong. His particular passion is the west coast of Scotland and her mountains in the winter. As well as an author, sea kayak designer and manufacturer, he is also an enthusiastic yachtsman. Howard's top ten sea kayaking tips?

- [ ] **Choose your expedition paddling partners carefully, especially if you sleep in the same tent as them!**
- [ ] **Don't use crap gear. If you can't get exactly what you want, modify something or make it yourself.**
- [ ] **Don't waste your money buying composite carbon-fibre or Kevlar sea boats. Spend the cash you save on another piece of good-quality equipment.**
- [ ] **Don't be afraid to say no. The outdoor environment is no place for egos.**
- [ ] **Remember the six Ps: poor planning and preparation produces poor performance. (There is a seven Ps version, but I'll let you figure that one out yourself.)**
- [ ] **Whenever you're on the water, no matter what your ability, ensure you're a totally self-contained unit, ie you can look after yourself if you become separated from your group and can deal with most eventualities.**
- [ ] **Water and rope (even a towline) is a dangerous combination. Make sure you always have a sharp, usable knife to hand.**
- [ ] **If you want your gear to last in a saltwater environment, make sure you wash it all thoroughly after each use. This has to be the worst aspect of all sea paddling.**
- [ ] **Spending some money on quality instruction/coaching (no matter what the activity) is always a good investment and will allow you to progress far quicker.**
- [ ] **Do everything you can to protect the environment we operate in, otherwise we'll lose it. For ever.**

HELEN WILSON

Helen Wilson specialises in traditional paddling skills using traditional equipment. She has competed in the Greenland National Kayaking Championship twice, receiving five medals in four disciplines. Helen performs rolling demonstrations, presentations and instructs at events worldwide. She has written skills articles for several publications including *Sea Kayaker* magazine, *The MASIK* and *Ocean Paddler* magazine, in which she has an ongoing feature. In 2010 she released an instructional DVD, *Simplifying the Roll with Helen Wilson*, which is available worldwide. She also serves as a board advisor for Qajaq USA. Helen is a certified yoga instructor, and Yoga for Paddlers has become a popular class through Greenland or Bust, the business that she runs with her husband Mark Tozer. For more information, visit www.greenlandorbust.org.

⬇ Helen Wilson demonstrating a balance brace in a traditional kayak, using only her balance and the buoyancy of her *tuiliq*, and no assistance from the paddle or the *norsaq* which can be seen under the decklines in front of the cockpit.

Here are Helen's own thoughts regarding sea kayaking: 'Being on the ocean is magical. The smell of the water, the feel of swells moving underneath you and the deep heartbeat that seems to generate through every wave all adds to that magic. For me, being in a skin-on-frame kayak that I built with my own hands connects me to that magic on a very deep level.

'Although I enjoy all aspects of sea kayaking, it was rolling the kayak that initially became my passion, and possibly a bit of an obsession as well. I would take my skin-on-frame kayak to the lagoon and roll for an hour or so. No matter how tense I was from work or the stresses that life can toss at you, by the time I was finished rolling I was relaxed and in an almost meditative state. The Greenland rolling competition list provided good guidelines, and it wasn't long before I'd worked my way through the list. At this time Greenland was still a faraway place, and because of finances I didn't even consider going.

'My friends, however, had other plans, and it wasn't long before the community had raised the funds for my first trip to Greenland. In 2008 I competed in the Greenland National Kayaking Championship in Qaqortoq. It was one of the most incredible experiences of my life so far. The championship was started as a celebration of Greenlandic culture, and I felt lucky to be able to participate in that celebration. In 2010 I returned to the championship again, this time in Nuuk, and this year my husband Mark Tozer and I will go again, and we'll experience Greenland in a different way as we guide an expedition on the East coast.'

The traditional paddler often prefers a slimmer and lower kayak with a tiny cockpit. Modern incarnations may have increasingly large cockpits for safety reasons, but for warmth and practicality of use a small round cockpit is king. The volume issue is also a modern phenomenon. High-volume kayaks feel safer in rough water but this is mostly an illusion, and they're more likely to be pushed around by wind and waves. The Inuit knew this and kept the volume to a minimum, thus saving a lot of materials as well.

The most iconic aspect of traditional paddling is the Greenland-style paddle, very long and thin with no feather. The blades are also symmetrical, not in the normal sense but in that the front and back of the blade is identical, though some people use an Aleutian-style blade instead, which is very similar but has a drive flat or slightly concave face with a rib on it a bit like a Euro-style paddle, and a convex back like a Greenland blade. This feels good because it gives a more confident drive stroke but maintains the very smooth sculling action that's a feature of the Greenland shape.

Greenland paddlers also favour the storm paddle, a very short version for use in high winds or choppy conditions. Generally they adopt a sliding hand technique to get extra leverage from such a short paddle, with one hand holding the blade and the other the middle. This may have been where Edi Hans Pawlata got the idea for the extended grip roll, since Inuit paddlers rolled like this in many circumstances.

Some also adopt the *norsaq*, a harpoon throwing board, because even if you don't want to harpoon anything this device, tucked under the decklines, can make a very effective backup paddle or rolling tool.

I should also mention the *tuiliq*, a waterproof coat with a hood that seals around the face and a hem that attaches to the cockpit of the kayak. Some traditional paddlers make these out of waterproofed canvas instead of sealskin. They're also available in neoprene wetsuit material and in hi tech breathable fabrics, and are a very convenient replacement for the sometimes over-complex apparel systems that modern sea kayakers use [see picture left].

⬆ **The small, round 'ocean' cockpit favoured by many traditional kayakers. Warmer, and easier to seal with the sprayskirt or *tuiliq*.**

⬇ **Sliding the hand to grip the blade.**

KAYAKS IN THE SURF

It always gives me great pleasure to remind surfers that kayak surfing is probably a far older activity than surfing on a board. Without a doubt the Inuit learnt to surf their kayaks many thousands of years ago, and we have archaeological evidence that the *caballito* craft of Peru were surfed with a twin-bladed paddle at least 3,000 years ago.

Today, however, we live in a world where surfboards dominate the waves, and we'd better not forget it. For better or for worse, board surfers are in the majority pretty much wherever you go surfing, and the manner of their surfing, if not the craft itself, isn't really negotiable.

Surfing 'properly' in a kayak is a very difficult skill to master. We must also be mindful of the fact that unlike most surfboards, a kayak is an equally dangerous projectile whether there's someone sitting in the middle of it or it's navigating the waves alone.

Because of this, my first rule of surfing is: do not *ever* take a kayak out in the surf if there are other people inshore of you, unless you're an expert and there's no possible way that you're going to lose control of said kayak or let it get away from you. Second rule of surfing: do not surf on a break where other people are trying to surf, until you've mastered the basics of catching a green wave, riding it in the generally accepted way, and getting off it when it breaks. My third rule? Know your limits. Yes, if you've taken your kayak to the beach to try surfing, you really *really* want to get in the water. But for everyone else's safety as much as your own, don't bite off more than you can chew!

So, what's the generally accepted way of surfing? Well, you must catch the 'green' part of the wave, once the wave has started peeling or breaking. Not before. Waves don't generally break right across the beach/reef at once. They start from one point, and the leading bit of the white water, as it progresses across the face of the wave, is called the 'shoulder'. You must ride along the green part of the wave (power pocket), next to the shoulder (it's the steepest, highest energy bit of the wave), until there's no more green left and the wave is all broken. And then get off the wave. Don't ride the white water to the beach. If you need to go ashore to the beach, bide your time and paddle in on the back of waves, so that you're in control of the kayak at all times.

Hmmm, this all sounds a bit onerous, doesn't it? You're probably asking yourself why you can't just mess about in the waves having a good time, doing whatever you feel. Well, you just can't, OK? Unless there's no one else around. Because if you don't surf in the accepted way, people will shout at you, and possibly even wait for you on the beach and express their dissatisfaction in a wide variety of ways, up to and including physical violence. I've seen this. So play nicely like everyone else.

Don't get me wrong. I don't want to discourage you from taking a kayak out in the surf. But I do want you to know how important it is to respect the etiquette of the waves. If you do so you may find that the surf zone is one of the funnest places you can be in a kayak, and go on to attempt some truly radical and wonderful things.

← This is modern surfing. Across the face of the wave, close to the breaking section.

↑ *Caballitos*, traditional South American reed boats, first surfed thousands of years ago. And Peruvian fishermen still enjoy a wave or two today...

↓ You must be able to get your kayak off the wave. It's very important.

SURF KAYAKING

What is surf kayaking? To my mind, it's surfing a wave in the generally accepted surfing manner (see etiquette on page 88).
While you certainly can surf an ocean wave with a sea kayak, a general-purpose boat or a sit-on kayak, it's quite difficult to ride along the face in this way unless you're in a surf kayak.

Surf kayaks come in several different incarnations. Some of them are long and pointy, some short and surfboard-like. Many are made of plastic, but the best ones are made from lightweight hi-tech materials like carbon-Kevlar. They're often mistaken for whitewater kayaks, but the genres differ greatly. A surf kayak is very directional, and usually has a hull like a surfboard with a deck on top that doesn't overhang the hull. They also often have fins. However, the most significant differences are that the cockpit in the surf kayak is a lot further back and the tail is tiny in size and volume, making the boat quite unbalanced in displacement but better when planing.

It's just about possible to surf properly in a whitewater playboat or a sit-on-top. It might be easier to learn the basics of taking off, and riding across the wave with a forgiving craft of this nature. Make sure you do it somewhere safe and away for other people, though, and if you use a sit-on kayak, stay attached to it using a leash! Then transfer these basic skills to a more specialised boat. Nothing really matches the performance of a proper surf kayak.

↖ **An older design of surf kayak called a 'surf shoe',** ↗ **and the very latest type of high-performance boat.**

IMPORTANT SKILLS

Before surfing anywhere near other people, it's pretty important to develop a reliable roll. An upside down out of control kayaker propelled by a breaking wave is pretty dangerous, and not something anyone wants to see. Rolling is also one of the only ways a novice kayak surfer can easily and safely get off a wave.

The next thing to learn is how to take off on a green wave. This is pretty tricky at first. The wave needs to be steep enough that you can stop paddling after about three strokes and the boat will keep planing, but not so steep that the bow catches or purls and you're launched forward. This is called 'going over the falls' and it's best avoided, all in all. It's going to take a bit of trial and error, so make sure you try it when the waves are very small. There's no point whatsoever in practising catching broken (white foam) waves because (a) it's really easy, they just pick you up and throw you at the beach; and (b) a surf kayak is completely out of control on a broken wave.

Start paddling gently, directly towards the shore. Then as you feel the wave lift the tail, start paddling as hard as you can – but try to keep your body still and just use your arms. Yes, I know that's the opposite of what I've said elsewhere in the book. But it's important not to 'rock the boat' during these three or four take-off strokes. If, after five or six strokes, the boat doesn't seem to be accelerating down the wave, give up and try another wave. That one wasn't steep enough.

Once you're planing on the wave, you must turn and ride across the face in the direction the break is travelling. This 'bottom turn' is best achieved with a lot of lean and not too much paddle input. For perfect form, wait until the shoulder of the wave is right next to you before turning away from it. At first, make a bottom turn and then keep your weight committed to that upwave (seaward side) rail so that you carve up to the top of the wave and over the back. Keep your weight on a low brace on that side. Now you know how to get off the wave when you need to!

As you ride across the face of the wave, you can control the kayak

by 'trimming'. Very small weight shifts from side to side can move the kayak up and down the wave. Weight shifts front to back tend to have the opposite effect from what you intended (see 'Action and reaction', page 41). If in doubt, keep your paddle trailing gently in the water on the wave side of the boat. Most of the steering is done by leaning, once you're planing properly. The paddle is mostly used for balance – trying to steer with it just tends to slow you down!

As you get more confident, you may be able to 'top turn' at the top of the wave to create more dynamic top-to-bottom rides. To do this you need to roll the kayak onto its downwave (shore side) rail as it reaches the top of the wave. It looks and feels awesome. Top surf kayakers can generate so much speed 'climbing and dropping' like this that they can launch right into the air – this is called an 'aerial', and it's really the Holy Grail of surf kayaking.

To learn more about kayak surfing skills, take a look at my book *Kayak Surfing* (Pesda Press, ISBN 10:0954706102).

⬇ **The perfect wave and the perfect place to take it – you could ride in either direction from this 'A-frame' peak.**

CHRIS HOBSON

'I started kayaking at the age of four, with my Dad, who was a member of our local club, Blackwater Canoe Club. The club is based on the River Blackwater, so river paddling was my main discipline for eight years. He took me to my first surf kayaking competition at Easkey, County Sligo, when I was 12. My love for the sport has grown ever since.

'I started out in river paddling, and competing in boatercross river races and slaloms in local club leagues, as well as being on the junior Olympic development squad. However, I consider surf kayaking as my main competitive goal.

'Over the past ten years I've been travelling to many national, and international competitions representing Northern Ireland. I paddled on both junior and senior level, in which time I've been lucky enough to travel to many parts of the world.

'With the support from my local club – the Northern Ireland Surf Kayak Club – and many people around me, I was lucky enough to win my first Junior World Title in 2006, the World Cup in Peniche, Portugal. Following that I won the Junior International Class World Title in 2007, in Bakio, Spain. My most recent success has been winning the Open High Performance Class at the 2011 World Championships held at Jeanette's Pier, Nag's Head, on the outer banks off North Carolina, USA. This was by far the most amazing experience, one which really blew me away.

'I've been fortunate enough in my kayaking career to work for, and become partner in, Mega performance kayaks. I love designing, making, and surfing the best kayaks in the world. And to see people enjoying something you hand-crafted is a very humbling experience.

'In my view the best surfer is the one having the most fun!'

⬇ The aerial is the Holy Grail of kayak surfing.

⬇ **A racing ski slices through swells and choppy seas. Note the leash attached to the paddler's leg so that the boat can't get away from him should he fall out of it.**

(*Lucas Tozzi*)

SURF SKI PADDLING

A surf ski is rarely called a kayak, but I'm not going to overlook the genre on that account. It's a highly specialised and very fast sea kayak hull but made in a sit-on-top style, popular with surf lifesavers all around the world. Measuring 5–6m (16½–21ft) long and only 40–50cm (16–20in) wide, surf skis are extremely quick when paddled on flat water (only an Olympic racing kayak would be faster), and the fastest paddled craft over long distances on ocean swells. They track well but are less manoeuvrable and have less transverse primary and secondary stability than shorter, wider craft. Because of this instability, a surf ski (with an experienced paddler) is a very effective craft for paddling in big wave or choppy conditions. Its narrowness and length help it cut or punch through large surf. Many racers use wing paddles to paddle a surf ski – these paddlers are typically not skilful 'kayakers', so speed, and the ability to get back on the ski quickly when something goes wrong, is the focus. That's why they wouldn't use a paddle that's good for complex strokes and rolling, as a sea kayaker might.

Surf skis aren't to be confused with 'wave skis', which are a kind of high performance sit-on-top surf kayak with a lap strap to hold you down.

Some cheaper, heavier surf skis are made from polyethylene. Lightweight surf skis are made of composites like fibreglass, Kevlar, carbon fibre or a mixture. There are basically two types of ski, one known as the lifesaving specification surf ski ('spec ski') and the other being the long-distance or ocean racing ski.

Ocean racing surf skis differ from spec skis in that they're longer, have sharply pointed bows and under-stern rudders. The front of the modern lifesaving surf ski is often equipped with a wing or sponson to prevent nose-diving when surfing steep waves towards the shore. Ocean racing surf skis are also usually longer than long-distance racing kayaks and have less rocker than sea kayaks. An ocean racing surf ski will have more volume in the bow to provide buoyancy and a dry ride when punching through waves, a long waterline to make use of ocean swells, and a sleek, narrow shape to reduce water resistance, as well as enough stability to make paddling in rough conditions feasible.

Of course, the kayak was invented as a fishing boat, and in modern times it's proved itself again and again as a cheap and low-impact way to get to places that fish can be found. You can tow a mackerel line behind a sea kayak and fetch up your dinner every time. Or stick a rod under the deck-lines, and fish proper angling style wherever the mood takes you. However, in recent years the popularity of sit-on kayaks has spilled over into a huge upsurge in kayak fishing, because even without Inuit-style skills, these stable and practical craft make a superb platform for catching even quite large fish.

While you can, of course, fish from any craft, there are now sit-on kayaks that are designed specifically for fishing. Their equipment includes additional storage, rod holders, paddle parks and attachment points for decklines and other gear. They often have more comfortable seats and backrests than a basic sit-on boat too.

INLAND FISHING KAYAKS

Inland fishing kayaks are often manufactured with a 'disturbed pattern' or camouflage finish. This gives them a low visual impact in the rural environment, but makes them unsuitable for open water where they won't easily be seen by other boats, or in an emergency. Such kayaks are often used for hunting too, where the law allows, because their camouflage gets them closer to the quarry than would easily be achievable in any other craft.

If stealth is important to you, then it's an idea to learn to paddle quietly. The key to this is to put the paddle-blade into the water fully before you apply pressure to it, and ease off the power before you recover the blade at the end of the stroke. The other thing that can make a lot of noise is manoeuvring with basic entry-level strokes like sweeps and low braces. Go back a bit in the book and learn to do bow rudders and draws, and practise a lot of 'stirring' as described in that section. Those are the skills you need to move your boat around skilfully and silent as a ninja.

In some countries, particularly the UK, there are all sorts of rules about fishing on inland waterways, and people take them extremely seriously. So I'd suggest you definitely enquire about angling regulations before someone officious shows up and ruins your day.

FISHING IN THE OCEAN

Sea-going fishing kayaks can get you to the best nooks, crannies and sandbars to track down your chosen marine prey. They're usually brightly coloured for safety reasons, and that doesn't bother the fish at all.

While the stability of a large sit-on-top is quite important for a fishing platform, it's a reminder of why Inuit kayaks were very unstable. If your boat tries to stay aligned with the surface of the water when the water's surface is sloping at a funny angle then you'll be rocking around all over the place if the sea is choppy or has much of a ground swell. For this reason I'd recommend a boat with less initial stability if you can find one, unless you anticipate going out only on very calm days.

My other hot tip for the sea fisherman is to invest in a decent ground anchor and a sea anchor. A ground anchor is important so that you can stay in one place, where the fish are feeding. It'll generally keep the kayak pointed towards the wind or the current, depending which is the stronger. A sea anchor won't keep you in one place, but will allow you to drift while keeping the kayak's bow pointed towards the wind and waves. It'll stop the boat from surging around, or even trying to surf. Whichever type of anchor you use, if you want to point in a slightly different direction the trick is to run the rope from one side of the bow instead of right on the nose. This will allow the kayak to track off slightly in one direction or the other.

Remember that when there's a lot of current and you're ground-anchored, or strong wind on a sea anchor, that if you fall off the boat you may not be able to swim back to it. Consider having a leash. If you can, take a mobile phone in a waterproof bag, or a GPS rescue beacon. And have this on your person, not in the kayak!

← **Using legs on one side and a parked paddle on the other as stabilisers for a touring kayak.**

↑ **Low visual impact fishing on a sit-on kayak with all the fishing equipment, including spare rods, safely stowed.**

GENERAL SAFETY TIPS FOR KAYAK FISHING

I'm going to take it as read that the dangers incumbent with fishing itself are well known to you. The additional risks specific to fishing from a kayak are few, but the main one is, of course, entanglement. You can get in an awful muddle if you get yourself or your paddle tangled in your fishing lines. It's also important to keep everything lashed down or stuffed under the decklines or shockcords. Because a sit-on kayak is quite a flat platform, it's easy for stuff to get pushed overboard. Or, if you capsize, you might have rods and all sorts of paraphernalia floating around to get tangled up with.

Sea sickness and dehydration can be issues when fishing at sea or on a hot day. Make sure you're prepared for these eventualities.

RAFAEL ORTIZ

Rafael Ortiz, extreme kayaker and Red Bull athlete:

'It's a calling. We have to get out of our boundaries, we have to try what others don't, to find the limits of what's possible.'

www.rafaortiz.com

(Photo Alfredo Martinez/ Red Bull Content Pool)

ADVENTUROUS PADDLING

Few outdoor sports can boast the range and scope that kayaking does. There are so many different styles of adventurous paddling, and different environments to consider, from steep whitewater rivers to open ocean crossings, dangerous extreme paddling to playboating, and the subsurface gymnastics of the squirt boat. So it's no surprise that some boaters choose to move on from placid water paddling to something more demanding, both physically and mentally, perhaps becoming more rounded and expert paddlers or even specialising in a particular discipline.

Before attempting to learn any of the paddling featured hereafter, you should be competent at paddling your chosen craft on flat water, and familiar with all the basic paddling and steering strokes. You should be physically fit, able to swim at least 50m (55yd) vigorously, and capable of remaining afloat indefinitely in your buoyancy aid and other paddling gear. You should also be aware of the limits of your body and how to look after it. Paddling can be hard on you physically, so preparation such as warming up and stretching before, and warming down and stretching after, can save you from injury or time off the water.

Having said all that, the big difference between placid recreational paddling and the more adventurous is mostly in the mind. Beginners sit on or in their boats and paddle around, and very pleasant it is too. More adventurous paddlers tend to outfit the boat until they're wearing it like a pair of trousers. With experience you'll become part of the boat as soon as you get in it – no longer a human attached to a craft, but changed into something else altogether, a kind of amphibious centaur with the torso of a human and a hard but streamlined lower body.

Whether you paddle rivers or in the sea, this kind of thinking is very important, because dynamic paddling means reacting to the forces that act on the boat and the paddle. These are your only points of contact with the outside world. When you drive a car or ride a bicycle, most of your information comes from what you see and hear. You're not truly part of the machine. In a kayak, you'll come to *feel* – when something moves the boat or touches its outer shell you won't just see it happen, you'll feel it just as if something had touched your own skin.

If you read on, it's not so much about how to paddle your boat as about providing you with knowledge that'll enable you to consider more adventurous paddling in salt water or fresh, fair weather or foul! Don't let theory put you off, though. There's nothing like water-time, as long as you approach it sensibly and safely, so if there's paddling to be done, go and do it, and use this book as a reference to make sense of what you've learnt for yourself.

← **Rafael Ortiz drops the 189-foot tall Palouse Falls in eastern Washington State on June 24, 2012.**
(Photo Lane Jacobs/Red Bull Content Pool)

PETE ASTLES

Pete Astles is owner, designer and maker of tea at Peak UK Kayaking Wear, and has been paddling for over 30 years in boats of every shape and size. He's a member of the GB slalom and freestyle teams, event organiser, Himalayan river runner and now sea kayak explorer, who recently completed the UK's three peaks by joining the mountains by bike and kayak.

Pete's advice? 'Planning and preparation are probably the most important parts of any adventure. Do your homework before you go, study maps, charts and Google Earth. Plan all your food, equipment and clothing well in advance. It's a great build-up to going off on a trip, especially in the dark winter months. Also, get out and train on your local water, whatever it is, in the river, lake or canal. Test your boat and equipment – even your meal plans. That way, if something can be improved or changed you can do it before you go. If all your planning is done well and your research has been thorough, the trip itself will be a pleasure. Of course, a few unknowns will crop up, but that's all part of the journey!'

CHAPTER 4

MOVING WATER

Paddling on anything more than gently moving water requires a whole set of extra skills. Luckily what follows can help you to understand the thrills and spills of the more frothy side of kayaking.

HYDRODYNAMICS

It's super-important for a kayaker to understand a lot about the behaviour of water, but most of us don't have degrees in hydrodynamics or hydrology. Never fear: this section is a short-cut to all the things I can be bothered to remember about water, from a paddling point of view at least.

First of all here's something important about how your boat moves through the water. When you paddle the boat, the main thing resisting your progress isn't friction, as you might imagine, but the effort it takes to displace the future water that the boat is going to be occupying in a quantum moment of time. The harder you try to paddle forwards, the more you'll push some of that water in front of you, forming the 'bow wave' of the boat, until eventually you're paddling in the trough of a big wave of your own making and have an impossible mountain to climb. This is why you can accelerate to a certain speed, and then, even if you double your power output, you'll not be able to go any faster.

A long pointy boat will have a higher top speed than a shorter one, because it's bow wave is necessarily longer, lower and faster – but the effect still applies. You'll never get it to plane on the flat.

A short boat, on the other hand, will accelerate much more quickly. So over short distances, for instance when ocean surfing or whitewater paddling, the short kayak makes much more sense.

← **Pushing water and making waves: in a kayak you very quickly arrive at a speed that you can't realistically exceed unaided.**

↑ **In shallow water you will experience a lot more drag from the water.**

GROUND EFFECT

If you paddle your kayak in shallow water, the waves that it makes are affected by the bottom. This means extra drag. So boats are harder to paddle in shallow water. Any depth less that half a boat's length and you'll really notice the effect.

PLANING

Planing is much misunderstood. Planing is what happens when a boat is going fast enough that it no longer displaces its own mass of water. This is because at a certain speed the water is hitting the hull hard enough to lift it up, overcoming the weight of the boat and any other downforces it may have by virtue of its shape. On flat water this can only occur with enough propulsion (you'd need a motor) to climb over your own bow wave. But it can happen in some other ways too...

SURFING

Surfing is what happens when the boat is sliding down a steep enough slope to start planing without any power input from the paddler. It can be seen to happen on the face of an ocean wave, or a standing wave in a river. But equally it can happen on the way down the back of a wave if it's big and steep enough!

BLASTING

Blasting is what happens if you're held in place by a hydraulic or breaking wave as the water travelling under it hits your hull. It feels like surfing, but it can happen without any gradient. In fact the boat is often pointing upwards while blasting water flowing down a drop.

There's also a common planing scenario which occurs when you're held sideways by a breaking wave or hydraulic. This is akin to blasting, but for some reason it's almost always called side-surfing. Or bongo-sliding. I couldn't tell you why.

BOOFING

When you land on the hull after a drop or flight of any sort, the impact initially generates a planing mode, and you'll travel forward planing for a short time if you have any forward momentum already.

ROCKETING

If you paddle head on into a jet of water, whether from an eddy into a current or a current into an eddy, the relative speed of the future water added to the speed of the boat can be enough to lift the hull into a planing mode. This can be utilised to get an accelerated phase, or to 'rocket cross' or 'rocket move'.

CURRENTS

Contrary to appearances, the currents in most rivers don't flow that fast. That's why a kayaker who can only travel at about 7mph maximum speed, can usually, if not actually paddle upstream, at least cross the current, without losing too much ground downstream. By paddling up eddies and crossing currents it's often possible to 'eddy-hop' upstream. This is sometimes called 'attaining'.

Currents in the sea are caused by tidal flow, and although they look more sluggish they can be a lot faster than river paddlers are used to. I've seen currents of 25mph in places of huge tidal range (see the Bitches fog story on page 140). There's no ferry-gliding across that.

WAVES

Waves in the ocean are caused by wind blowing across the surface of the water. Once the wave is large and in motion, it will travel far beyond the reach of the wind that made it. But the water doesn't travel, it just moves up and down. Only the wave energy and elevation actually travels across the sea, as a 'swell' or 'roller'. When the wave gets to shallower water, which could be a sloping beach, a shallow reef rising out of deep water or a vertical cliff for that matter, the wave energy won't be able to move freely and the wave will 'break'. The more sudden the transition, the more violently that will happen.

Waves in a rapid happen because the water itself is moving, and when it hits an obstruction, ledge or a shallowing of the riverbed this generates some vertical energy and makes a stationary 'standing wave', or a series of them called a 'wave train'. Just like the ocean waves, if the water is shallow or constricted enough the wave will break. The difference is that river waves don't form, break and reform – they are what they are, and they stay in one place as the water moves by.

HOLES

If the wave is breaking hard enough it's called a 'stopper' or 'hole'. This commonly happens as the water pours downwards after a drop. 'Hydraulic jump' is the technical hydrological term for this. But it can be observed on the surface too. The important thing to notice is whether white water is being recirculated strongly upstream. If it is, it can stop or hold a kayak. If the recirculation is deep and powerful it can hold a less buoyant object like a swimmer. Learning to read holes is an important skill if you're going to paddle on white water.

It takes experience, but here are the important factors. If the hole or stopper runs right across the river, you'd better be sure you can punch

through it. Or if it doesn't, but the ends are upstream of the middle, you'll struggle to paddle out of it. If its ends bend downstream it'll probably be easy to escape, or just slide off either side, even if it's really big.

Holes and waves on a rapid often overlap. This looks hard to read, but there's a really easy trick. Look for the downstream Vs formed by adjacent waves. Paddling down the V as if it was an arrow pointing the way is almost always a safe route. Just make sure it isn't pointing directly at some hazard before you set off! Otherwise, just cruise from one V into the next for a smooth, slick-looking line down the rapid.

BOILS

As the water struggles to squeeze itself through constrictions and complicated topography, it kind of spills up and out wherever it can. Water rising to the surface like this looks as if it's boiling. It's actually like a giant mushroom of water, flowing up the stalk bit and then spreading out on the surface and sinking down at the edges [see photo above]. Viewed from the top, it's a big patch of water flowing outwards and sucking down at the periphery. It's a nasty phenomenon, snatching at the edges of your boat and, if it's big enough, threatening to suck the kayak under.

POUROVERS

A word of warning. A pourover is the kayakers' name for water pouring over a boulder in the current. It's a matter of scale, as little ones don't do much, but if there's a lot of water pouring over a rock like this, the hole behind it won't be fun. Pourovers are easily spotted, making a distinctive round-looking wave as you approach from upstream. Waves aren't round, so alarm bells should ring. Ironically, once the boulder is covered with deeper water and stops looking like a round wave the hole downstream will often be a nice friendly one to play in. So it's all about the telltales.

GRADING WHITE WATER

Whitewater rapids are 'graded' on a scale of 1 to 6 (or I to VI), using a system known as the International Scale of River Difficulty. Rafters, kayakers and rescue services all use this system as a quick and easy way to describe the severity of a rapid. Some people call it the 'class' system, classes 1 to 6, but it's the same thing.

It's not a very scientific method, but it's been around for a long time, and most kayakers understand what you're talking about if you use it.

I should say from the outset that you can't give a grade for a whole river. It refers to individual rapids, and even then it's common to see a '3(4)', for instance, meaning that the rapid is grade 3 but there's a bit in there somewhere you'd have to call a 4.

GRADE 1

Small waves only, clear, visible passages, no serious obstacles. A beginner could float down this sideways with only basic flatwater skills.

GRADE 2

Moderately difficult waves and hydraulics, visible passages, any obstacles easily avoidable. A beginner could negotiate this forwards using basic flatwater skills.

GRADE 3

Intermittent but powerful waves and hydraulics. Rocks, eddies, passages clear though sometimes narrow and not necessarily visible without manoeuvring. An expert would run this effortlessly without needing to inspect it from the bank, but an intermediate would need to inspect the rapid, make a plan, and then execute it carefully using practised whitewater skills.

GRADE 4

Long continuous rapids with powerful waves and hydraulics and dangerous rocks and other hazards. Scouting advisable first time down. Powerful and skilful manoeuvring required. Experts only. Some experts are still flippant about grade 4, but it's getting close to the limit. Intermediates often attempt it and usually struggle or fail.

GRADE 5

Super-difficult. Long, continuous, violent rapids. Route extremely obstructed. Big drops and fast currents – inspection essential but often difficult. All safety precautions must be taken. Even the most expert kayakers look at grade 5 with some trepidation and then run it with care. If you swim (ie fall in), your life is probably in serious danger.

GRADE 6

The upper limit of possibility. Unpaddleable for almost everyone. The absolute extreme of every conceivable feature. Probably only one route that will (might) work, and that route has to be followed inch-perfectly. In other words, you swim, you die.

↑ How would you grade this rapid, having read how to do it? I'd say it's grade 3. Pushing 4, but not quite. An expert could just about read the line from upstream and the holes and waves are not really that powerful. With a bit more water, though, it could go up a grade...

GRADING VERSUS DIFFICULTY

The grade of a rapid is always going to vary with the level of the water. This doesn't mean higher is harder. It usually is, but sometimes a rapid 'washes out' at high water and becomes easy, and sometimes very low levels make it technically very difficult to manoeuvre, and perhaps expose new dangers like siphons. On the other hand, big volumes of fast-moving water may sometimes not require much skill, but could pose serious risk of injury or death if you swim.

There are various different and very specific wordings of the 'international' system published by the authorities in different countries, but wherever you go in the world the basic concept of each grade/class of water should be pretty well understood by kayakers.

Some people annotate the grading with a plus or minus to add a bit of fine detail. So '4+(5)' would mean a hard 4 with a bit of 5 in it. '3-(4)' an easy 3 with a little bit of 4. For me, this smacks of trying to be precise about something that's inherently imprecise, but people do it, so I thought you should know!

ALEX RODEGRO

Alex was born in Lippstadt, Germany, in 1977. He describes the city as a 'little stronghold for kayak slalom athletes'. He started paddling when he was three, and slalom racing when he was eleven. After an illustrious career competing at the top levels of German slalom kayaking he took a break to study architecture. When he returned he was, as he puts it, 'infected by the disease of creek-boating'. He now regularly travels the world hurling himself down the spectacular rapids of Norway, Switzerland, Austria, Portugal and Chile, as many incredible photos attest. You can follow some of his adventures, and those of his friends, at www.nookiecompany.blogspot.com.

Alex runs the 'Devil's Throat' drop on the Rio Claro in Chile.
(Seppi Strohmeier)

WHITEWATER BOATING

Going back a few years, or perhaps decades, when I first became interested in whitewater kayaking, there were two main arms of the sport. Paddling your kayak down an exciting river, whatever its grade of difficulty, was called 'river running'. Playing around doing tricks was called 'playboating'. And very often the two were one and the same thing. For a while, everyone used boats that were, broadly speaking, slalom kayaks, but then there was a radical phase of development that made playboats very different from river running boats. Undaunted, many of us carried on using playboats to paddle difficult white water, but eventually they were just too slow and uncomfortable, and they were downright dangerous on shallow, bouldery streams. And so the 'creek' boat was born, to address the needs of people who liked paddling playboats but needed something bigger and safer to run narrow or technical whitewater rivers, and it's lately become the accepted choice for all downriver paddling, even on big volume water.

↓ **Alex drops some classic Norwegian rock.** *(Michelle Basso)*

ON RIVERS WITH FRIENDS
BEN WHITE

'As the sun dipped briefly below the horizon in northern Norway at around 1:00am, the four of us stood looking down over the river unravelling itself below. We'd been on the water for a few hours by this point, and it had already been far tougher than we'd anticipated. The line through this rapid was long and complex, requiring a few 'must make' moves at the top in order to line yourself up correctly to avoid the undercut rock at the bottom. Safety cover was hard to place and could only be effective from the bottom of the rapid, which meant the first person down was on their own! Losing 'rock, paper, scissors' (the only fair way to decide who goes first), I was up.

'One last mental run-through of the line, then with shaky hands I heave my spraydeck on and into the flow. Move across to follow the wave train, punch the guarding hole, a well-placed paddle stroke to stay high on the slab, boof the landing and paddle hard to stay out of the tow back. Slalom through a rock section, sprint for the lip of the last drop, lift a knee, pull hard on the paddle, take off. Silence. Land hard, edge right and push away from the undercut. Safe!

'I signal to the guys it's good to go. One by one we assemble at the bottom to watch the last man down. He's on a mission but ricochets off a rock near the top, spinning him off-line through a big hole and he's out of his boat. Without a word we get him a rescue line, yank him out of danger, and two of us jump in our boats and give chase to his gear. Eventually catching up with the waterlogged boat, we disturb a moose and her calf crossing the river. We share some time on the river, as she looks on, bemused by the bright plastic, before continuing the crossing and vanishing into the undergrowth. The other guys blatantly don't believe us when we share the experience (might have something to do with emphasising how dangerous they are when with calf!), but just in case, all stomp off down the bank making lots of noise to retrieve the rest of the gear.'

2007 World Champion Men's Freestyle Squirt Kayak, boat designer and all-round nice guy, Ben says that his favourite things about kayaking are 'working with the power of the water to smoothly flow from one line to the next, using every river feature to play your way downstream, and finding the calm when split seconds last a lifetime as the maelstrom rips around you!'

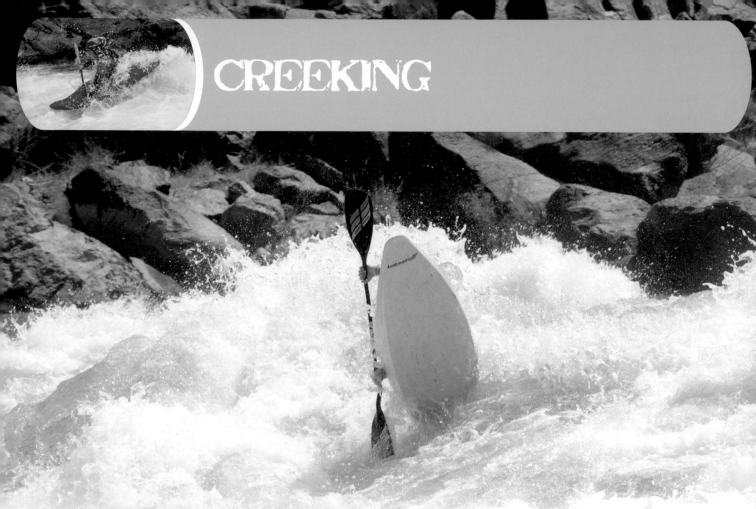

CREEKING

reeking has become the common expression for downriver whitewater paddling. Although the word 'creek' means different things in different dialects around the world, the 'creek boat' is the standard weapon of choice for the whitewater paddler, and so the type of kayaking you'd use one for is generically called 'creeking'.

To understand creeking we need to take a look at different types of white water. It might help to consider two examples. The first is 'big water', where the difficulty derives from the sheer volume of water fighting to squeeze through the riverbed topography. The other is steep technical water, where the gradient and the narrow gaps between the rocks or banks is the main challenge for the kayaker. The former is normally characterised by huge waves and holes, and fairly unstable and transient eddy lines, whirlpools and haystacks, whereas steep creeking is all about manoeuvring the boat between boulders, through tight and complex channels and over drops and waterfalls, all the time dealing with the turbulent interaction of fast water and rock.

These two examples are extremes. Some of the most challenging whitewater falls halfway between the two. It's perfectly possible to find water that's steep, technical and big volume. Or to experience both kinds of paddling on the same river. And remember that waterfalls can be found on any river, whether it's narrow and technical or big volume and wide. Look at Niagara Falls, for instance!

The current (!) state of kayak development tends towards using the same kind of kayak or 'creek boat' for all downriver paddling. Although for a while it was accepted practice to use short manoeuvrable boats for technical streams and longer, fast ones for big water, it's become clear that acceleration – a feature of shorter boats – is ultimately more important than speed on a rapid. Which is a great relief to those who paddle a lot of different rivers but don't want to own a whole quiver of boats. Today's creek boat is a high-volume short boat that can be used for any kind of white water.

Creek boats have a raft (I'm so funny) of safety features that are pretty important on white water. The handles at each end of the boat are made from sterner stuff – they aren't just for carrying or hanging the boat, but for rescuing it from rapids or when it's pinned by the current. There may also be other handles, called 'broach loops', to facilitate such rescues. Many paddlers utilise these to construct an arrangement of webbing to help them climb out of the boat unaided if it becomes entrapped.

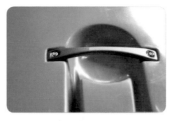

The footrest of the kayak will be a reinforced plate that doesn't allow the feet to go past it, and it may include some sort of shock absorption system. This is pretty important when impacts – either with rocks or vertically into the water – are a fairly regular occurrence. A lot of padding inside the boat, and airbags to keep it afloat when swamped and maintain it's structural integrity under pressure, will complete the outfitting.

Finally, the plastic shell of the kayak will itself be extra thick and reinforced, to reduce the chances of it breaking if it hits a rock. Having said this, you should know that the manufacturer will take a dim view if you try to make a warranty claim because you broke the boat this way. Nothing is indestructible, especially you. So try to navigate the rapid, not bounce from rock to rock.

EJ JACKSON

Eric ('EJ') Jackson's biog details succinctly summarise the man and his lifestyle. Born 1964 in Rock Island, Tennessee. His favourite place to paddle? 'With my kids, Rock Island, Zambezi, Nile, Ottawa, Costa Rica, California, uh… everywhere.' Crazy fact about EJ? 'Sorry, I can't hear you. I'm deaf.' Why EJ loves kayaking? 'The river is loud, rambunctious, unpredictable, and beautiful, like my wife and kids. The river is a dependable soul mate.

'I'm so lucky to be surrounded by many of the world's best paddlers. We all have more fun in one day than many people have in a lifetime, it seems. We're lucky, blessed in that way, and driven.'

The stats read something like this: EJ has won the biggest international freestyle competition of the year for six out of the last ten years, including three Men's Pro World Championships, two Men's Pro Pre-World Championships, and one World Cup for Men's Pro (he also won the 1993 World Championship). He took a silver medal twice in the Worlds, in 1997 and 2009. He also has a long history of extreme racing, winning most of the Gorge Games (Upper White Salmon, Oregon) races, for both extreme and boatercross, as well as many Great Falls races, and more. Olympics and slalom are in his background too, with USA Team appearances from 1989–98 (though he didn't make the 1993 team).

EJ also designed, with his design partner David Knight, the freestyle kayaks that won the 1999, 2001, 2005, 2007 and 2009 world championships.

MOVING WATER

PLAYBOATING

Playboating is all about showing off – doing tricks on (usually) safe rapids, using the power of the water to perform aerial or sub-surface gymnastics in your kayak. It looks crazy, and it kind of is... but it's oh so much fun!

Play paddling is the name we kayakers give to doing freestyle tricks on whitewater rapids, either on the way downstream or by surfing one particular wave or hole. The latter – if one can simply drive to the river, play on a wave and go home again without having to shuttle or run any rapids – is often known as 'park and play'.

Generally, when we talk about play paddling we're referencing the use of 'playboats', kayaks which have been specifically designed for the purpose. Stunt kayaks, if you like. But you can play in a creek boat or a GP boat to some degree, and on occasion people have been known to experiment with acrobatics in sea kayaks and slalom boats. Kayakers are a naturally playful crowd.

The first kind of play paddling most people attempt is surfing a wave. This is a difficult skill to learn, but if you start on small waves and work up you'll find yourself able to control the boat on some real monsters!

← **The author playing in some whirlpools in Val Sesia, Italy.**

↓ **Surfing a micro wave.**

→ **2011 World Freestyle Champion James Bebbington and a gigantic river playwave.**
(Katya Kulkova, riverzoo.com)

**↑→ Paddling out from
an eddy on to a fast,
surging wave.**

Playing in a hole or stopper is a slightly different matter. The hydraulic will hold your boat, and you have to concentrate on staying upright and in control. Having said that, the tricks that skilled playboaters can perform in such features are truly astonishing.

Eddy lines are also good for play paddling. The classic move is the tail squirt, also known as a pivot turn [see photo below].

Once you can do a range of different moves, you'll find it interesting to try to link them together into sequences. Some sequences flow nicely together into a sort of gymnastic ballet, and end up being given crazy names like Tricky Wu and Phoenix Monkey. This is the beginning of freestyle paddling as seen in competition.

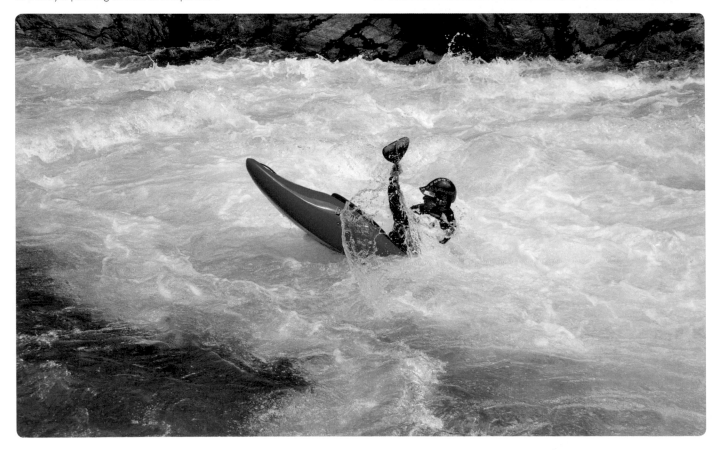

PRINGLE

James 'Pringle' Bebbington was born in 1986. He started kayaking when he was nine or ten and was hooked from the get-go:

'I started out playing around on lakes and in the pool, then moved up to small rivers in Lancashire and Wales. Then, as my paddling progressed, I took a couple of coaching courses with my local shop to teach me the fundamental skills of whitewater. I gradually moved on to paddling more and more whitewater in North Wales and the Lake District with my canoe club. I was about 13 when I first saw freestyle kayaking in a magazine. Straight away I knew that was where my passion would be. I saved up my pennies, doing every odd job I could scrounge from my parents and neighbours, until I got my first boat. I never looked back, and have been paddling hard around the world, playing, competing and enjoying the freestyle lifestyle ever since. Now I'm a seven-time GBR Freestyle Kayak team member, British Champion, World Champion, World Cup Champion and European silver medallist. I'm training harder than ever and enjoying it more and more.

'As a young paddler I was desperate to learn all I could, and be on the water as much as possible. I dreamt of being a World Champion. My first struggle, though, was getting comfortable upside down... I was determined to get over this fear. I knew as soon as I beat that fear I could really enjoy surfing and running rivers like my idols at the time. It took a while, but I kept throwing myself at it and soon enough I got used to it and got going properly. The first lesson I learnt? Never give up! At the time my dream of being a World Champion didn't really seem possible, but over the next 13 years I just followed my heart. I paddled as much as I could. I never listened to those who told me I needed to get a "real" job. I just kept doing what made me happy.

'I eventually focused harder on my skills and looking after my health. I work on all my moves, both sides, wave and hole. I work on my fitness. I compete as often as possible. Sure enough, three years of this training and lifestyle paid off, and I won Worlds! Simply by doing what I love, working hard and focusing a little!

'My advice for all young rippers is to get out as much as you can, get lots of competition experience, look after your health, be positive, and never let your dreams get away from you. They are possible!'

⬆ The loop (basically a somersault) is a favourite hole trick with play paddlers.

⬇ Pringle performing the kind of complex 3D aerial move that make him a World Champion.
(Katya Kulkova, riverzoo.com)

SQUIRT BOATING

← **As you can see, the squirt boat is so low-volume it barely floats...**

Like so many things in this diverse sport, squirting was invented by many people at different times in different places. But the art of sinking one end of your boat was first harnessed by slalom paddlers, who discovered that using stern-dips could make them go faster. As Jim Snyder wrote in his excellent publication on the subject, *The Squirt Book*, the move has now been absorbed by the realm of fun, but science should get the credit for it. Once upon a time someone coined the term 'squirt' because of the way the boat squirts forward as the sunken buoyancy of the stern resurfaces, and the rest is history.

While a lot of kayakers have found reason to learn the stern-dip, it's only ever been the lunatic fringe who chose to paddle super-low-volume boats. Largely because of the influence of the Snyder brothers in the '80s, the boats grew smaller until they had to be custom-built to fit the owner. With minimal volume the boat became almost invisible to aerated water, and responded only to the power of the green. This allowed the pilot to navigate the intricate subtleties of the river's currents. While squirt boats gave us the ability to cartwheel, blast and splat in our plastic boats, the latter, cruder craft will never be able to enter the total access mode of river paddling. Significantly, though, it helped less lunatic folk realise that you could play your way down the river, rather than running a river with freestyling interludes. Because squirt boaters play the whole run.

Before squirting was invented in the '80s there really weren't any specialist playboats. Freestyle tricks were honed and defined in all-round whitewater boats like the Mirage, and were therefore pretty much limited to loops, surfing and paddle twirls and throws. Squirtists showed the way, and, although it took over a decade, the kayaking world eventually got specialist freestyle boats that could do some of the things squirters had invented, and for a while we all ran rivers in these low-volume playboats, because it was so much fun.

Ironically, it is arguably the popularity of freestyle that has sent squirt boating back into the shadows. Once people could do cartwheels in a relatively comfortable plastic kayak, the appeal of the original was lessened somewhat. And then in a more sinister development – in the same way as paddle twirls were suddenly laughable once we had acrobatic tricks like cartwheels to attempt – the cartwheel became a bit of a joke amongst freestylers, and that was really the squirt boat's hallmark move. Now that most playboaters are only interested in air moves on waves, the influential nature of the squirt boat is no longer apparent. Attempts to make planing squirt boats that can do the new-school stuff just resulted in kayaks that were rubbish at all the rest of the squirt repertoire, and still not as good on a wave as a playboat.

Squirt boating is now even more of a lunatic fringe than ever before, then, not least because the remaining proponents have an unhealthy obsession with 'sinking', or what used to be called the 'mystery move'. This involves using the current to disappear completely below the surface, sometimes for scarily long periods of time, before popping up way downstream.

Squirt boating still gets a lot of respect from the old-timers of whitewater boating, so it's unlikely to disappear from freestyle events, despite not really being on the new-school radar. But even if it does go, the lunatic fringe will still be there, albeit in tiny, isolated groups like some dissipated Jedi, a constant reminder that the paddlers of these glittering slivers probably invented every freestyle move except bouncing.

ACCESSORIES AND CLOTHING

In addition to the gear suggested in the earlier part of this book, there are a few specialist pieces that every whitewater paddler should consider.

NEOPRENE SPRAYSKIRT

Probably the most important upgrade for paddling in rapids is a very good neoprene sprayskirt. This will usually be quite tight and have a rubberised coating on the underside to make it stick to the cockpit rim. These decks are hard to put on and remove, so aren't suitable for beginners or those of a nervous disposition, but in rapids it's important that there are no leaks and that the skirt won't suddenly come off at an awkward moment. Such sprayskirts are also usually reinforced around the edges to fend off knocks and pinches from rock or paddle.

ANTI-IMPLOSION BAR

Some sprayskirts have a stiff bar across them to make it pretty much impossible for the skirt to collapse under the force of the water. Personally I have reservations about this – I've heard of people injured or entrapped by this bar when they were swimming. A sprayskirt can be implosion-proof without this feature. Sometimes, though, the skirt does get pressed in and cause the boat to lose volume, which can be a bad thing. One solution to this is the overthruster.

➔ Invented by playboaters wanting more 'pop', the overthruster is a plastic pod placed under the sprayskirt. It increases the volume of the boat and supports the sprayskirt, but can be jettisoned if you need to bail out.

BUOYANCY AIDS

While many kayakers venture on to moving water with much the same buoyancy aid as they've always used, it's as well to consider having a little more protection. Whitewater buoyancy aids tend to have more all-round impact protection, particularly at the shoulders, and some extra reinforcing. They also often have pockets to carry essentials you wouldn't want to lose along with your boat. You'll see a lot of paddlers with buoyancy aids that have a built-in harness and other rescue features, but this isn't something you need until you're ready to learn how to use them properly, or paddling on serious rapids – over grade 3, say. Wearing the thing and not knowing how to use it can cause more problems than it solves. There's a detailed explanation of the features of such buoyancy aids in the 'Whitewater safety and rescue' section.

HELMETS

You can paddle white water perfectly well in the sort of plastic helmets that you're issued as a beginner, but they usually have holes in them that let trees and water in, and sit away from the skull, which allows the river to try to tug them off your head. Most whitewater paddlers consequently use a close-fitting helmet made from hi-

tech composite materials with a foam lining. They're rather expensive and need to be replaced after any serious knock.

Some extreme paddlers even like to use a full-face helmet similar to those designed for downhill mountain biking and extreme skiing.

NEOPRENE LEGWEAR

Although it's common to wear drysuits or other shell layers when paddling, one shouldn't overlook the importance of leg protection. If you take a swim in even quite mild rapids, your legs can get pretty bruised and bashed. In more serious water you can get an absolute battering. Neoprene legwear helps a lot (well, a bit), worn on its own or under a drysuit or dry pants. Many kayakers favour three-quarter-length designs, because they're so much easier to put on and take off, and pretty much reach down to sock/boot height anyway.

DRY TOP

The dry top, dry cag or 'dry paddling jacket' (what a mouthful) is a pretty ubiquitous piece of clothing among whitewater boaters. It's like the top half of a drysuit, so it has drysuit seals (or very good neoprene ones) at the neck and wrists and waist, and no need for a zip. In most other situations you'd prefer something with more ventilation and comfort, but in rapids the priority is to keep water out of the kayak, even if you don't mind getting wet yourself. The dry top makes a good seal against the sprayskirt (some are even joined to the skirt) so that, assuming it doesn't leak, your boat won't fill up.

Or you could wear a full drysuit. It's best to get one that's designed for kayaking specifically, because these have an outer flap/tunnel/waistband that covers the sprayskirt tube, and stops water from simply flooding down the top.

ELBOW PADS

In narrow, technical or just rocky rivers, it might be worth thinking about investing in a pair of elbow pads, or a dry top that has them built in. One smack on the 'funny bone' and your paddling skills can be quite compromised. Or you could even break your elbow.

THROWLINE

Even if you aren't skilled at using a throwline, it's a great idea for everyone in the party to have one about their person, if only as a washing line or to drag your boat up (or down) a steep bank. But why not learn to use it? It's a bit of fun and you can practise in the back garden. And you might save someone's bacon. For more details on throwline use, check out the 'Whitewater safety and rescue' bit.

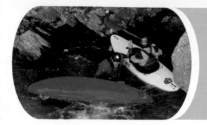

WHITEWATER SAFETY AND RESCUE

Just as we need to learn some extra special paddling skills before we can feel comfortable on moving water, there are some things everyone should know about safety and rescue. The whitewater environment in particular has its own special hazards, and everyone should know about the basic techniques and equipment.

ROLLING

Most people venture on to white water for the first time before they learn to roll. Indeed, it's usually this experience that prompts them to learn to roll! But if you can reliably right yourself after a mishap, you'll enjoy your paddling a lot more. And I suggest that you work on a combat/front deck roll, that keeps your head tucked up and out of harm's way, sooner rather than later, because you'll normally default back to your first roll if you practise it for too long.

SWIMMING

Kayaking in white water is awesome fun, up to the point where you leave your comfort zone and it gets very scary. Swimming in white water is rubbish, pretty much right from the outset. You just get beaten up by rocks, and it's incredibly difficult to keep your head above water.

If you find yourself swimming in white water, get on your back with feet pointing downstream. Keep your feet up. Use them as shock absorbers to push off any rocks. Keep hold of your boat and paddle, if you can, because these help you float, carry you through hydraulics, and you don't want to lose them. Wait until you're rescued or have a chance to catch an eddy.

If you realise that you're going to go down a dangerous channel, or for any other reason you need to bin the boat and paddle and get out of the river, then turn on your front and swim directly across the current to an eddy or low rock or exit point, and don't stop until you're safe.

TOWING

Don't use a towline. You may have found them useful on flat water or in the sea, but don't use them in white water. A sling around your elbow can be a good tow if you're very confident. Otherwise, only tow people or boats by having someone hold the back of your kayak.

ENTRAPMENT

Entrapment is the number one danger in moving water. Boats and people are easily pinned by quite moderate flows. Usually they can only be released by pulling directly upstream, but vertically upwards is worth a go too.

THROWLINES

The throwline is a standard and very ubiquitous piece of rescue equipment amongst whitewater kayakers. It's often said that every paddler should carry one, although I'm inclined to say concentrate on basic whitewater confidence first. You should definitely carry a throwline once you know how to use one and have a sporting chance of being able to assist in a rescue. But it's nevertheless handy if everyone in the party has one, as I've mentioned before.

⬆ **Throwing a throwline from the bank to someone in the river.**

A throwline is basically a floating bag containing floating rope. You can throw it to someone in the water, while keeping hold of the other end of the rope, and arrest their downstream progress or draw them to safety. It's worth practising this as much as you can, because when your friend needs help is no time to be trying to figure it out! Some people are very good at throwline rescues, and some are hopeless, and the difference is mostly experimentation and practise.

The principle of throwline use is this. If you're on the bank, you can rescue someone from the river. Undo the bag, pull out a couple of metres (6ft) of rope, shout to get their attention, and then throw the bag past the person. Don't throw it at them – they stand much more chance of getting hold of a big, long rope across the river than a small bag. And don't let go of your end! Bring the rope around your back and brace yourself for a big pull. If other people are around get them to hold on to you as well. Wait for the current to swing the victim into the bank or an eddy. Never attach the rope to anything in this type of rescue.

OK, those are the basic basics, but if you're serious about white water then go on a rescue course or read a book about this. Try *White Water Safety and Rescue* by Franco Ferrero.

Many throwlines are rather over-engineered for most people's needs. Get one that's light, compact and specifically designed for whitewater use, with a rope thickness of 8mm or more and at least 15m (50ft) in length. But don't worry about crazy strength specifications unless you're trained in swiftwater rescue and know that that's something you need.

A lot of people store a throwline in their kayak, but the very best way is to wear it around your waist on a purpose-designed belt. This keeps your hands free for climbing and clambering until you need to deploy the line. I like to wear mine in front but under my sprayskirt, as it doesn't get in the way, and that's a bit of a dead space in a kayak.

In conjunction with your throwline it's often useful to have a couple of climbing slings to help attach it to things, or for towing or tethering, and some climbing or marine karabiners. For reasons I'll explain later, screw-gate locking karabiners are the safest, but there are other useful types, including one that's designed to clip around paddle shafts. With this basic selection of gear you can rescue a lot of situations. Finally, though, if you have ropes you should always carry a knife. A folding one is safest. I tie mine to a piece of string to avoid losing it, but don't tie the other end to your buoyancy aid or the like – that's a recipe for falling into turbulent water and getting cut up by a flailing knife. You're better off losing it!

Golden rule of rope rescue, accepted by professionals and enthusiasts alike: never attach anyone to a rope or anything else unless they have the means to release themselves from it if they want or need to.

Golden rule of whitewater rescue, courtesy of humorist William Nealy but absorbed into rescue folklore: never by your actions put yourself or the victim in more danger than the victim was already in.

HARNESS BUOYANCY AID/PFD

There's rarely been a piece of equipment so ubiquitous yet so little understood. Just as most whitewater paddlers are aware that it's

⬇ **A throwline being used to rescue a trapped boat.**

➡ **Taking the strain with the rope held around the back.**

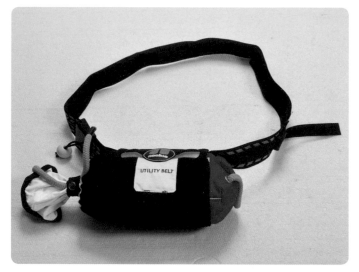

↑ The professional way to repack a throwline, feeding the rope into the bag so that it won't tangle.

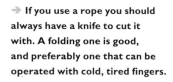

↑ A utility belt can be used to retain a throwline so that when you get out of the boat and run, your throwline comes with you hands free.

→ If you use a rope you should always have a knife to cut it with. A folding one is good, and preferably one that can be operated with cold, tired fingers.

accepted practice to carry a throwline, many also feel that it behoves them to purchase a specialist whitewater buoyancy aid (sometimes called a personal flotation device or PFD). However, aside from the questionable benefits of a large pocket or two, the features and function of such safety products are lost on many.

← A typical harness rescue BA/PFD, complete with chest rescue belt.

Design

Of course, the primary function of a buoyancy aid is to do nothing. The more it feels as though you're wearing nothing at all, the better mobility you'll have, and this, of course, helps you to paddle better. With this in mind, all high-end vests/jackets are cutaway designs with the distribution of foam kept away from areas that might impede body rotation, leaning, and arm movement. And since we hope to spend 99% of our time paddling and not swimming, this is pretty important.

The second most important function is location. The shell, straps and other closures have to be designed to keep the BA/PFD in place, with minimal ride-up when swimming. This doesn't include the big fat seat-belt-like strap round the middle. This item, usually called the chest belt, is NOT intended to assist with the fit. More about that later.

The third most important function is swimming. You should be able to adopt a defensive swimming posture (on your back, feet downstream) or an active swimming posture (head up breaststroke or front crawl) with equal ease. If you can't switch between these, you're helpless in a whitewater swimming scenario.

The third most important function is impact protection. While the designers work hard to allow great freedom of movement, they're also cognisant of the ever-present threat of impact from rocks, timber or boats. The most common whitewater impact injury is clavicular (collar bone), hence the major padding in that area, which also helps you to carry your boat; but the ribs, kidneys and spine are major areas of vulnerability that also receive consideration. At the time of writing there's nothing your buoyancy aid can do to prevent shoulder dislocations, so I suggest you learn to low-brace, avoid poser-ish behind-the-head strokes, and take any swimming impacts on the buoyancy aid or better still feet first, to avoid the instinctive 'shoulder charge' response that can ruin your paddling career.

Finally, after all these issues have been taken care of, the designers go back to the drawing board and build in dynamic rescue features. The primary one of these is the harness. This is a structure of webbing that runs from the waist over the shoulders of the product, and is intended to ensure that the buoyancy aid cannot be ripped apart in a forceful rescue. If it's well designed and uninterrupted by weak points like buckles, it can up the shoulder strength of the BA/PFD from around 75kg to 500kg or more. There will also be a chest belt running around horizontally, which has a variety of different functions and is, importantly, removable.

Strength – shoulders

Basically you should *never* try to rescue someone by the shoulders, but if that's the only thing you can reach, you're going to give it a shot, aren't you? However, countless people have had their shoulder straps broken by would-be rescuers, and even with a super-strong design that's intended for whitewater rescue, a really strong pull can rip the buoyancy aid clean off the victim, leaving them with nothing. So, if you have any option at all, steer clear of the shoulders and take hold of the chest belt or the back of the buoyancy aid below the shoulders.

Strength – sides

The sides of all buoyancy aids, even the basic ones, are very strong. It's part of the EC regulations for selling them. So this part isn't going to break. Even if you have no chest belt or harness to get hold of, grabbing the buoyancy aid just above this and pulling from the back should minimise the chances of pulling it off.

LIFTING FROM THE BELT

Lifting or pulling someone using a correctly fastened chest belt is the safest way of all to extract them from the water, as long as their chest belt is correctly fastened. If it isn't, all that'll happen is that it will come undone, and the person should be in no more danger than they were in the first place. Which as we've seen is one of the basic rules of swiftwater rescue. If grabbing them by hand, take hold of the belt wherever you can, but probably the most effective way is to grab both sides of the chest belt under the arms. In a mechanical rescue using ropes, cowstails and/or karabiners, the attachment point must only be at the centre of the back where indicated. So now I've opened a whole can of worms – I need to explain what I mean by 'correctly fastened', and also a bunch of issues to do with the location point at the back. So here we go. (Don't skip this part, it's an important bit!)

Locating at the back

On the back of your rescue BA/PFD, whatever the design, there will be TWO retaining straps in the middle (which may or may not be part of the harness structure), with the chest rescue belt threaded through them. The only correct place to attach anything is between these, as shown. Some versions come with a welded steel ring, or there might be a cowstail or sling attached, or many serious pros just leave a screwgate karabiner permanently attached at this point.

➔ **This guy is a raft guide/whitewater rescue professional, and is equipped with a harness BA/PFD and a throwline stowed in a utility belt. Note the screwgate karabiner attached to the centre back of the chest rescue belt. Clearly, he is dressed for warm water conditions.**

BUCKLE AND FRICTION PLATE SAFETY OPTIONS
ALWAYS TEST THESE ON YOUR BUOYANCY AID/PFD BEFORE USING IT IN THE WATER

■ Ignore the friction plate and just go straight through the buckle. This has the advantage of making the buckle lie pretty flat, but the belt may well slide through the buckle under load, or the buckle may break at the plastic lugs/pins on each side, depending on the manufacturing tolerances of the buckle and webbing. Which isn't a good thing to stake your life on. It would be embarrassing to drown because a £1 plastic buckle turned out not to be manufactured to aerospace standards, because it never will be.

■ Thread the belt through one slot of the friction plate, and then through the buckle as shown in the photo. This system is probably not going to slip until you experience forces way in excess of those that'll prohibit breathing and probably injure you. At which point you probably want it to! And because it takes most of the load on the plate and the edge of the buckle, it doesn't load those skinny little plastic pins much, so you're unlikely to have a catastrophic failure.

■ Thread the belt through both slots of the plate and then through the buckle as shown in the photo. This system is never going to slip, and might be considered for a situation where coming off the rope would definitely be fatal. It's a pretty difficult two-handed operation to pull the belt out of this set-up, even once the buckle is undone. So, I don't think anyone really wants to get involved in that, do they? Really?

The steel ring probably won't fail, but there's no way of knowing because there's no industry standard rating system for welded rings, so personally I throw them away.

The cowstail is all well and good. But if you use one, make sure the attachment at the back is a screwgate. Otherwise bad things can happen, namely that a free-gate karabiner can take a knock and attach itself to pretty well anything. Usually the retaining straps on the BA, sometimes worse. It's scary, and potentially fatal, so don't risk it.

Towing from the chest belt

OK, a lot of people do this but I have to say it's frowned upon. Towing anything from the chest belt means there's a danger of getting in a tangle if you capsize or the towed thing gets hung up on something. Although the chest belt is technically releasable, it doesn't just fall off you when you release it, so that can be a problem too.

If you tow a heavy thing, like a waterlogged kayak or a sea kayak and paddler, then the load is applied to your back very high up, and this causes difficulty in paddling and possible injury to your back. So all in all I'd suggest getting a proper tow belt, as they're very cheap and avoid all those problems.

Threading the friction device/brake plate/load spreader

Right, I've touched on this throughout, but now it's time to explain what it's all about. Or maybe earlier on in the chapter was the right time. And may still be. Anyway, see photos.

Point number one: there's a lot of disagreement among paddlers about how to thread the friction device on your chest belt buckle.

As usual, most people are wrong, some way or another. Am I being arrogant? No, I'm being a bloke who designed and tested whitewater rescue BA's for over a decade. So listen up.

Point number two: there's a lot of different information from manufacturers about the correct way to thread the friction device on your chest belt buckle, even though they all use broadly similar, or in some cases identical, components. Why is this? Well, I don't know to be honest. But let me just say that I never attribute to conspiracy what can reasonably be explained by incompetence.

So I'm going to suggest that you ignore everything anyone says, including me, until you've tried all three ways of threading your buckle and friction plate that I've described above. On dry land. Don't start messing about in the water. That'd be crazy. Once you know how it performs, then you can make informed decisions.

You may have worked out by now that my choice of set-up is number two. I never use any other, because you don't always know in advance when someone else is going to clip something on to you. If I'm definitely not up for any kind of rescues, of me or others, I take the belt off completely. Otherwise I use number two. Make your own decision.

Before using a rescue BA/PFD equipped with a chest belt, it's essential that you seek instruction from someone experienced and competent in swiftwater rescue, or go on one of the many swiftwater rescue courses that are available. Until you've practised using and releasing your chest belt in controlled conditions, I recommend that you remove it completely and leave it at home.

RIVER SCOUTING FAIL

The Plym used to be my local river, and at that time it was regarded as one of the most challenging runs in the UK. At 300ft per mile with no large vertical falls, it's steep, bouldery and siphon-packed, unrunnable at low flow, super-technical at medium flow, and absolutely terrifying in big flood.

My friends and I paddled it regularly. We all knew that you should scout blind drops, but if you did that on the Plym you'd be there all day – there's a blind drop every 20m! This was maybe the first run since some heavy rain, and we were on the lookout for new timber and strainers in the river – but not so much that we were going to get out of our boats. So we exercised a little caution and stretched our necks a lot, but not a great deal else.

Patch was the first in our group to run one particular narrow drop. I saw the tail of his boat disappear, and then immediately a turbo backender. He rolled up in the pool looking a bit shaken but didn't signal any problem. Still, I thought, there must be a sticky hole, and attacked the lip with some speed myself, although it wasn't really a boofable drop. The result was that I took the log in the chest even harder than he did, same turbo backender, same roll facing upstream. I tried to wave a stop to Pete, the next guy in line, but it was too late, he did the same thing. It was only when there were three of us in the pool, waving the stop signal, that the rest of the group got the message and took a different line.

The moral of the story is, scout everything, no matter what a pain in the neck that might seem. Ninety-nine times out of a hundred you'll curse the time wasted. But there could have been any number of unhappy endings in that tree.

→ If you can't see properly what lies ahead, always get out of the boat and scout on foot, to make sure you can run it safely.

WHITEWATER TECHNIQUE

I'm going to go out on a limb here, not for the first time, and assume that because you're reading this book rather than watching a video about it online, you're pretty intelligent and open-minded. So I'm attempting to approach the fundamentals of swiftwater paddling very differently from anything I've seen before. Most instructional resources have a very systematic, even dogmatic way of taking us through the basic techniques for getting around on the river. They talk about how to move into the current from the safety of an eddy (breaking in), and how to escape from the current to an eddy (breaking out). They also describe the two main ways of moving across the river, the ferry glide and the S-cross. But I'm going to try to describe a more holistic way of doing these things, so that instead of puzzling over which tool to use, we can be a little bit more flexible and understand the whole thing properly.

Fast moving water tends to come in discrete chunks. It isn't (usually) randomly swirling about – viewed from the surface there are slabs of water moving downstream, upstream or staying still. It's always a huge revelation to the uninitiated, to stop, empty the mind, and truly see what's going on in the flow. So, these slabs of moving water don't really like to mix together. Where they meet there'll be an interface line – sometimes called an eddy line, wall or fence – where the two slabs rub together but retain their own integrity. It's a bit like plate tectonics, this! At the interface, there may be a bit of friction and this might cause whirlpools, or the line might wobble around a bit, but basically the slabs behave themselves and stay intact. They might, under extreme duress, start to bend and break and form waves, but they only disintegrate when they get a proper smashing, after a significant drop or what hydrodynamicists call a 'hydraulic jump'. And they soon reform downstream into another selection of slabs, rubbing shoulders with each other on the riverbed.

Kayakers use the expression 'future water' to describe the bit of water they're going to be in next. It's a useful way of thinking. If you do nothing you'll stay embedded in the same piece of water as

← ↓ **This sequence shows just the right angle of attack and amount of lean for entering a moderate current from an eddy.**

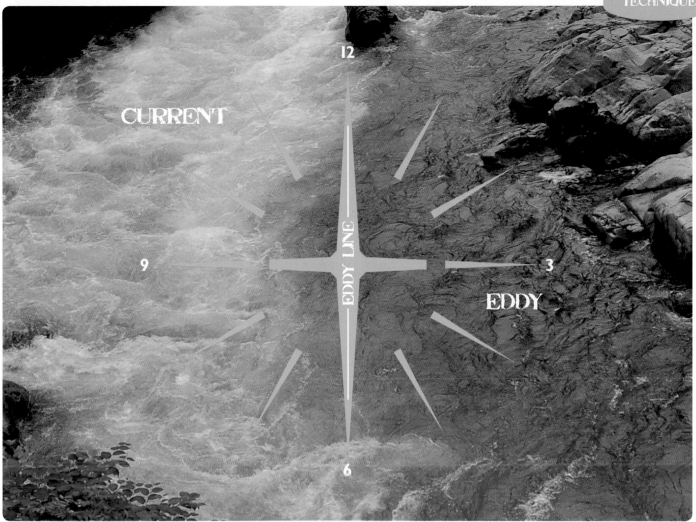

CURRENT

12

EDDY LINE

9

3

EDDY

6

it does whatever it's doing. Going downstream, for instance. So think about the next piece of water. The future water.

When you negotiate this seemingly complex world in a kayak, the name of the game is go with the flow. If you want to go downstream, try to be on a slab of water that's going downstream. If you want to stop, get on to a slab that's stationary. And if you want to go upstream, you can often even find a bit of water that'll facilitate just that. But what you must learn is how to make the transitions between these many discrete chunks. Which is, if you like, a quantum leap.

What you need to do is stop thinking about your ground speed and think only about your speed relative to the slabs of water. Once you've got your head around that, you only need to worry about two things: critical angle of attack, and critical angle of lean.

Now you're on your own – because the actual angle depends on what boat you're paddling, your weight, and how fast you're going when you hit the eddy line. So you're going to have to start by imitating other people, and then find your own best practice from experience.

The key thing is this. As you move from one slab to another, the end of your boat entering the new slab will be carried along in whatever direction the 'new slab' is going. But the bit on your boat that's still in the 'old slab' will be going with that bit of water. So it isn't hard to see that you may get spun around.

What's less obvious is that there's a rotational force applied to the boat in a tipping-you-over kind of way, and you need to learn to lean

the boat over in anticipation so that the current in the new slab hits the bottom of the boat, not the side. Not too much lean is required, but if you don't act before this happens there's no way to save it once the water grabs you. You'll flip for sure.

What this means in a nutshell is that you must lean upstream before and during entering an eddy, and downstream if you're leaving one. Simples. In order to feel confident doing this, you'll need some support from your paddle, but that's handy because it's on the right side for the type of steering you're going to want to do in all circumstances. It's almost as if someone designed rivers to be great for kayakers. Or kayaks to be great on rivers.

But let me tell you the following as an approximation, and because no one likes a maths lesson I'm going to use the numbers on a clock face instead of degrees and stuff.

If we assume the eddy line runs from twelve o'clock to six o'clock, angles of attack up to five minutes before or after (as appropriate) will probably get you across the line without spinning around. Angles of five to ten before or after will get you across, but you'll probably spin around to point the opposite way. More oblique than that and you definitely will. As I say, you can affect this with your lean and speed, so practise.

If you try to slide in at less than five to or five past the hour, so to speak, you'll probably bounce off the eddy line and not make it. Or be left floundering on a wobbly bit of water with different things happening each side of you. Which is confusing, and not that much fun.

BREAK IN/OUT EXECUTION

It's a common mistake, but you don't have to lean over a long way to make the move stick. Doing this is usually counterproductive and leaves you in a tenuous position on the eddy line.

Now, I'm going to reiterate that before any part of your boat crosses the line, you have to apply the appropriate amount of lean, as shown in the photos. I usually set the angle of attack with a forward sweep stroke, since you do need forward speed, and then activate the lean. The balance and/or turning stroke on the inside can be anything. I generally use a low brace. Slalom racers and people who don't want to waste time getting on to the next power stroke use a bow rudder. And people who really aren't sure what exactly is going to happen next usually just keep paddling with a combination of sweeps and power strokes, to make sure that what they wanted to occur actually does!

I was shown a really good exercise when I first started whitewater kayaking, and I'd like to share it with you. I haven't seen people practising it for many years, but it taught me a lot about edge control, and anticipating what the water's going to do to your boat.

↑ **Paddling out of the eddy and into a gentle current (flowing right to left). You only need to lean/edge the boat a little bit.**

Find an eddy – start with a gentle one. Then poke the bow of your boat across the eddy line into the current, and try to stop with your body right on the eddy/current interface. The current should carry your bow one way and the eddy will push the stern in the opposite direction. Help this along with gentle strokes, and see how long you can keep spinning before you reach the bottom of the eddy. Keep the boat fairly flat unless you feel the water grabbing at the rails at one end more than the other.

When you're really happy with this (it does tend to give you a bit of a warm glow inside), try it with more powerful eddies, and try also to do it without using your paddle. The trick to this is moving your body (see 'Action and reaction', page 41) to keep the boat on the eddy line.

Once you're good at moving between slabs of water, and being comfortable on the unpredictable interfaces, you can try to link up different moves.

⬆ **Crossing a more dramatic eddy line, this time from the current (flowing right to left) into an eddy. The kayaker has applied quite a lot of edge!**

➡ **Spinning on the eddy line (which runs roughly centre top to bottom of the photo) using mostly the current differential alone.**

↑→ **An S cross sequence, leaving an eddy on one side of the river and immediately carving into another on the opposite bank.**

CROSSING THE RIVER

There are really two ways to cross the river: the S-cross and the ferry glide.

An S-cross means breaking into the current on one side, heading briefly downstream, and breaking out on the other. It's no different from breaking in and breaking out again on the same side, except that it's on the other side, so it forms an 'S', and sometimes you need to change edges quickly in the middle. Doing this smoothly looks and feels really cool. But never be bamboozled by it. You're just doing two things you can already do, one after the other.

A ferry glide looks easier, but it's harder. You must cross the current without letting it spin you around. The trick here is a very narrow exit angle, maybe eleven or one o'clock, and keep the upstream rail smoothly elevated with no wobbles. Keep paddling and adjusting your angle so that you go neither up nor downstream and you'll steadily track across to the other side of the current.

Practise it from eddy to eddy at first, and later on you'll find yourself using it more in mid-current. Sometimes you'll also need to do it in reverse, facing downstream and back-paddling. The reverse ferry glide is the ferry glide's even more difficult younger brother. It's an incredibly tricky thing to learn but it's used all the time to reposition yourself on the river and line up with where you need to be.

If there's a convenient wave across the river, you can try to paddle on to the upstream face of that and try to surf across. This is one situation where playing and surfing skills really come into their own.

The classic ferry glide fails are: too little angle, and you end up paddling straight upstream; or too much angle so that you veer off and head downstream. The angle between these two scenarios is very small, which is why ferry glides take a lot of practice.

JET CROSS/ROCKET CROSS

I lied. There's actually a third way of crossing the river, which is like a 'cross' between a ferry and an S-cross. I call it a jet cross or rocket cross. To be honest I'm not sure if anyone else does, but a lot of good paddlers use it and I have to call it something. It's a good move if the water between the eddies is super-fast, perhaps a powerful 'jet' coming out of a drop or rapid that would be too fast to ferry and perhaps an S-cross would be a bit out of control too.

The plan is this. You attack the jet with enough speed up the eddy that the boat instantly begins to plane. You then keep paddling enough to keep it planing for the few seconds (and it'll be very few, believe me) that it takes to plane right across the river. You don't need much edge control for this move, but do keep a bit of edge on (towards your destination), because if you wobble on to the other rail at this speed you'll shoot back into the eddy you just left.

So, let's re-emphasise the important points of whitewater technique:

■ The golden rule is always lift an edge to present the bottom of your hull to the approaching water.

■ Moving from current to eddy – lean upstream. From eddy to current – lean downstream.

■ When ferry gliding, tip the boat so that the upstream edge is slightly elevated.

There's one exception to the first rule, and that's when dropping into a breaking wave. In that situation you need to lean downstream, on to the wave. What this effectively means is you should probably lean downstream in most situations. Here's a little mnemonic: 'If in doubt, lean downstream; breaking out, lean upstream'. Keep that in mind and you won't go far wrong.

OK, that's quite enough to think about... go out and try it!

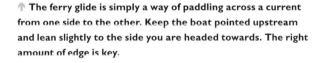

↑ The ferry glide is simply a way of paddling across a current from one side to the other. Keep the boat pointed upstream and lean slightly to the side you are headed towards. The right amount of edge is key.

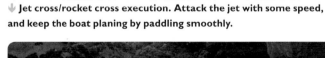

⬇ Jet cross/rocket cross execution. Attack the jet with some speed, and keep the boat planing by paddling smoothly.

RUNNING RAPIDS

The route taken by a kayaker down a rapid is usually called their 'line'. So, how to choose an acceptable or even comfortable line? Well, there are a few ways. Follow or imitate someone more experienced maybe. But beware, that person's line might be reliant on some skills that you don't have. So think about that!

If there's no one to follow you can work out a safe line, to the next decent eddy at least, by reading the water from the boat. It takes experience, but it can be done. Just look out for hidden 'horizon lines', somewhere there's a drop and therefore some stuff you can't see. Furthermore, there's no point in seeing a safe path to an eddy if there's

no viable way on from there. So you need to keep your wits about you when reading from the kayak.

Best of all, get out on to the bank and walk the whole section, so that you look at every feature from upstream and downstream. And then upstream again. That friendly-looking wave is actually a killer pourover? Well, who knew...

Where possible, stay in the green. If you can do that all the way down the rapid, threading your way between the white bits by following the downstream Vs, then you'll have a dry (and safe) ride. That's not always possible. Sometimes there is no dry line, except the one down the bank. So you have to decide whether to walk, or to negotiate the features of the rapid that you can't avoid.

The main things you're going to have to deal with on the way down a rapid are waves and holes. Waves aren't a problem, unless they're huge or breaking hard. If they break and reform, watch your timing so that you don't arrive just at the moment it all falls on you. If they're big

⬇ **The safe route through this turbulent rapid is clearly shown by the 'downstream V'. Either side of it lie breaking waves, rocks and hydraulics.**

THIS IS THE DOWNSTREAM 'V'

⬆ **Rule of thumb for holes. If you couldn't get out of being held sideways, don't go in at all.**

⬆ **If you can retain your balance, and paddle out of one end, then it's all good.**

⬆ **But sometimes it's hard to hold your upstream edge out of the water and the current grabs at it, and might flip you upstream.**

and very steep take a diagonal approach. Most green waves in rapids are shaped like pyramids, so paddle over one side rather than right over the peak.

Holes are best avoided if you can go around them, or jump over them. If you can't, then speed is your friend. You can try to punch through the hydraulic, but if you can lift the boat up and over the pile using body language, then it's much better than taking the hit in the chest. But don't do it if you'll leave your tail deep in the flow, because then the force of the water will hurl you end over end. It's all about the shape of the entry compared to the shape of the boat. You'll learn to judge for yourself – probably after getting it wrong a lot of times. My rule is, if I don't think I'd be able to retain control and paddle out of a hole if it held my kayak side-on, I'd rather not risk going in there in the first place.

⬆ **This paddler has blundered into the 'meat' of a hole and gets a slap in the face and a huge backender for his trouble.**

⬇ **This boater has used good timing, body language and direction to avoid the worst of it and jump diagonally over the pile.**

You might wonder why all the fuss about eddies. Well, unless a river is made up of single drops followed by long sections of slack water, which is rare, eddies are the only way you can stop for a rest, a regroup, or to give yourself a stern talking to. For that reason eddies are pretty important to whitewater paddlers, and so there's a bit of an international etiquette and protocol as to how they're used.

If you're the only person on the rapid, knock yourself out. You don't have to think about anyone else, and you can descend it swooping and whooping with joy at the elegance of your skills. Well, that's what I like to do. If there are other people with you, you have to think about them too.

On rapids that are fairly easy for your skill level, it's normal to paddle down together, and all stop together in a large enough eddy from time to time. This means that the lead paddler must think about the size of the eddy, because if he stops in one and there isn't room for everyone, that will commit some (maybe less experienced) paddlers to looking for their own eddy downstream. On super-hard rapids it's more usual to paddle from eddy to eddy one at a time, so only one paddler is on a rapid and exposed to danger.

Normal practice is to aim for the top (upstream end) of an eddy.

⬆ **Two paddlers in the slack water of a large eddy, looking upstream. The current is flowing from left to right of the picture, on the other side of the large rocks forming the eddy.**

This usually has the most defined bit of eddy line and hence a cleaner transition into the slack water. The exception is when the eddy is feeding powerfully back upstream, because you don't want to get pushed straight back into the current at the top. Anyway, normally you enter the top of the eddy and then back away from the eddy line to allow the next person room to get in. And so on. There's nothing more annoying than someone who sits on the eddy line watching you approach from upstream. Do this to an experienced paddler and he'll just curse and go around you – do it to a beginner and he'll probably park his boat on top of you. Because he really wants to be in that eddy!

Unless you can manoeuvre around each other in the eddy there's a good chance that whoever was first in will be the last to leave when it's time to push on downstream. This is one very good reason to place the two best paddlers first and last in the group. The order of the group can just reverse each time you all eddy out together.

MICRO
EDDY

CURRENT

TOP
OF EDDY

EDDY LINE

SLACK
WATER

BOTTOM
OF EDDY

TURBULENCE

↑ Playboaters call this a wave with 'eddy service'. While one paddler is playing on the feature, the others can wait their turn in an eddy next to it, without being washed downstream.

↓ Going for a micro eddy. There isn't room for the boat to spin around in the actual eddy, so you have to be quick and precise.

EDDY SERVICE

Sometimes, when there's a decent-sized eddy next to a play spot of some kind, paddlers will be waiting in line to take their turn on the feature (which will usually be next to the top of the eddy). This is called 'eddy service', and it turns river-running etiquette on its head, because it's rude to jump the line and dive into the top of the eddy. If

you're a beginner and plainly terrified then the paddlers in the eddy will make room for you, but will expect you to go to the back of the eddy queue afterwards. If you're not, then join the queue at the back to start with.

MICRO EDDY

A very small eddy with room for only one kayak in it is called a 'micro eddy'. They're hard to hit accurately enough to make the move stick, so are usually avoided by beginners. But strong paddlers will often use them to break the rhythm of a descent or just to spin around and check on the rest of the group behind, or to let someone catch up. It's a lot smoother and more effortless than back-paddling and looking over your shoulder, let's say. A move like that is sometimes called an 'eddy turn'.

DEATH EDDY

A death eddy is a type of excessively powerful eddy in a difficult corner that you can't paddle out of easily or from which the exit isn't into safe water but straight into some sort of trouble. Sometimes (often) they fill up with debris, fallen trees and other stuff all swirling around you. Don't be so desperate to eddy out that you make a bad choice like this.

EDDY-HOPPING

It's important that you don't commit to running more of a rapid than you can see or know is safe. So each time you leave an eddy, have a plan for where you're going to stop next. This way of running rapids from eddy to eddy is called 'eddy-hopping' and it's a good way of breaking down the run into manageable chunks, short enough that you can visualise what you need to do all the way to the next stop. In a group, make sure everyone knows when you're leaving the eddy and where you're going next. Don't let people get into their own little bubble. It leads to tears.

RUNNING DROPS

Running steep drops and waterfalls is perhaps the most iconic type of whitewater kayaking. Paddlers who succeed in paddling big ones are some of the most revered athletes in any extreme sport genre, let alone just kayaking. This is because the immense preparation and skill required to have any kind of control over the descent is belied by the short moments it takes to plummet to success or doom.

There are basically two types of drops – sloping or vertical. They each have their unique set of problems. What they have in common is that most of the problems come to fruition at the bottom of the drop, so this is our first port of call when inspecting them. And you should always inspect them.

With a vertical waterfall, the main consideration is the depth. Can you be sure the water is deep enough that you won't hit the bottom if the boat dives in nose first? And if not, can you be certain you can land flat enough to avoid that? If you can't check the depth, using a paddle or a pole or by swimming around below the drop, then it's not safe.

The next thing to worry about is the height. Extreme paddlers like Rafael Ortiz have survived landings from nearly 60m (200ft), but for mere mortals 6m would present significant danger. Be realistic. Work up slowly and progressively to running the bigger drops.

Waterfalls usually have a deep and powerful hole at the base, and in some cases this extends backwards too, into an eroded cave behind the fall. Both things are very dangerous, but you'll usually land downstream of the hydraulic. Sometimes, through bad luck, it's possible to bounce or 'pop' back upstream into the danger area, so be sure you can get enough projection to avoid this, unless you're attempting a meltdown.

A meltdown is a way of running the drop so that your hull stays in contact with the falling water all the way down, so that you go through or under the recirculation at the base of the fall. This method was invented by squirt boaters in the 1980s and has made it possible to run bigger drops, but it's a low control scenario that can go wrong, especially in higher-volume kayaks. Just paddle towards your chosen spot on the lip of the drop. As you tip over the brink, move your weight smoothly right forward to kill any rotational momentum as you drop into the vertical. You don't want to land upside down! Keep your head down on the deck and the paddle along the boat so the water doesn't catch it. On huge drops some paddlers throw their paddle away to reduce the chances of breaking it or being injured by it. You'd better be able to hand roll if you're considering this.

You can attempt a meltdown on a sloping drop, but you need speed and luck unless you're in a very small boat!

BOOF

Boofing is the way most vertical drops are run these days unless the height precludes it. Drops over 8m (25ft) or so aren't really boofable, the risk of spinal compression is too great. It should be avoided on anything over 4m (13ft) unless the water is massively aerated to cushion the landing.

⬆ **Checking out a waterfall from the bank. Think about the depth, the approach, the line, and where each paddlestroke should be placed.**

⬇ **Leaving the lip of the waterfall with a strong 'boof' stroke to project the boat out from the base of the fall.**

RON FISCHER

Swiss extreme kayaker, river gipsy, kayak bum (his words, not mine!), running the waterfall known as 'Duck Slide' on the Rio Manso, Bariloche, Argentina.

'To dream is what keeps me sane, and to turn those dreams into reality creates happiness. Every life is a journey, and the road to walk is your own. These are the simple principles by which I live my life to the fullest.'

(www.ronfischer.ch – photo: Mariano Buenaventura)

The way to boof is to paddle very briskly to the lip of the drop, keeping the weight forward. At the very last stroke off the lip, take your body weight smoothly back with the stroke so that you shoot the boat forward horizontally from the top of the drop. Once you're in freefall, throw the body forward to keep the bow up and get the paddle away to one side. A low brace position is good. Otherwise the paddle tends to bounce off the water or boat and hit you in the face. You should land with a resounding 'boof' a good distance from the base of the fall, with a bit of downstream momentum.

→ **About to land a boof. The key is to land as flat as possible. Keep your paddle away from the boat because it can bounce off and break or hit you in the face.**

⬆ **The author paddles off the downstream 'point' of a complex drop. This ensures landing away from the complexities of the water pouring in from the sides.**

SLOPING DROPS

The problem with sloping drops is often the hole at the bottom, which can be disproportionately large. Whether you can pass through it easily depends on complex riverbed topography. But a good guess is this: if the wave/hole is straight across the river with no gaps or Vs in it and more than 60cm (2ft) high, then I wouldn't want to bet on it. As we've seen, even a small hole can hold a boat sideways, and running sloping drops straight isn't always easy.

If there's a pronounced downstream V shape in evidence, then aim for that. Another option is that sloping drops often have decent eddies at each side of them, and you may be able to do a sort of boof off the corner straight into the eddy.

COMPLEX SHAPED DROPS

If the lip of the drop itself is V-shaped in plan and pointing downstream, paddling off the point nearly always gets you past the hole. If the opposite, one of the downstream ends next to the bank is your best bet.

Multiple (two or more tier) drops are intimidating, but it's really a case of having a plan for each tier from the outset – as long as that plan doesn't go wrong, because you probably won't be able to stop between drops!

Complex multiple drops with twists and turns in them require a lot of thinking about. Sometimes it's best to send down a stick, a ball or even a boat with a cockpit cover on it first, to understand which way the water will send you. Even then it's a black art, unless you can see a clear path from one downstream V to another.

In all cases, assure yourself that there are no obstructions like hidden rocks or trees in the plunge pool before attempting a drop. Just because there weren't any last time, doesn't mean it's still safe now.

MORE ETIQUETTE, ANYONE?

There are quite a few important whitewater etiquettes in addition to being considerate about eddies. Here are a few that crop up pretty often:

☐ Whoever's paddling down a rapid has right of way over people who are playing, crossing or waiting, until safely in an eddy. However, if someone is playing on a wave or hole, it would be rude to set off from upstream of them knowing this will mean they're expected to stop and get out of the way.

☐ Anyone upstream of you can reasonably expect you to indicate that it's safe or otherwise to descend, or even give them some guidance about the best line, even if they're not part of your party. They can't reasonably blame you for being wrong, though.

☐ If someone is struggling or looks anxious, then make allowances for them. Let them get to where they need to, whether it's their 'right of way' or not.

☐ Always go to the aid of someone in trouble. No doubt it's been you before, and it will be again.

☐ Don't obstruct someone on their chosen line down a rapid. They probably don't have a viable plan B.

☐ Be equipped well enough not just to ensure your own safety, but to provide basic rescue and support to others.

☐ If someone swims, save the person, not the boat.

☐ Communicate clearly and often to make sure everyone knows what's happening. A whitewater rapid is a very noisy environment, and verbal communication is generally impossible unless the other person is in the eddy next to you. And sometimes not even then. There's no universally accepted system of signals so make sure your own group understands the signals being used, and run through them at the beginning of the trip. It's important!

SHUTTLE

Here's a thing that a lot of books don't cover, but it's a big part of kayaking and a source of much confusion to a lot of paddlers. The expression 'shuttle' is most commonly used by whitewater kayakers, but it's equally applicable to any journey by kayak that doesn't end up at the same place as it started. How on earth are you going to get back to the car? Or your dry clothes, or whatever?

Quite often, when you're on a kayaking mission, your mind will be focused on the problems or challenges you may face while in the boat, and so logistical problems on the bank seem bigger and more complex than they otherwise might!

Let's look at the simplest case. A group of paddlers is going to drive to point A, and paddle to point B. On arrival at point B, they will usually want to get changed into their 'land' clothes, and they'll want to load the boats and kit on to the transport to travel home. So, once everyone is ready to paddle, they need to 'run shuttle'.

Two vehicles must leave point A with all the dry clothes and anything else that will be needed immediately at the end of the trip. One of them will be left at point B with all of this paraphernalia, and the two drivers will return to point A in the second vehicle. At the end

of the paddling trip, the vehicle left at point B can be used to take as many drivers as necessary back to collect the vehicles from point A.

That's as simply as I can put it, and it already sounds a bit complicated, doesn't it? It really isn't, but it actually does take a while for the whole shuttle concept to become second nature.

If security is a problem you'll probably need to leave someone with the boats at the put-in, unless you want to mess about with locking them to a tree or something, and even then the paddles and kit are usually an issue. At the other end of the scale, if it's a really safe place it's possible to make a solo trip, returning on foot or by bicycle if distance and conditions allow.

The weather is also a factor in planning your shuttle. Depending on the climate, and the nature of your boating and the trip, you may have different things to consider. In warmer climes, perhaps you'd drive to the put-in wearing the same shorts you plan to paddle in, and drive home in them too. In other parts of the world you can pretty much expect that none of your kit is going to stay dry, even the 'dry' kit, and that no one is going to want to stand about in the rain or cold while you run the shuttle at the beginning of the trip. Even less so when everyone's cold and tired at the end!

Think about these things in advance. They're often much more important than what actually happens on the water. Get them sorted properly and you'll have a much more pleasant trip.

⬇ **To run a vehicle shuttle you need a minimum of one vehicle/person who is not kayaking, or two kayakers both with vehicles.**

CHAPTER 5

SEA KAYAKING

Sea kayaking is one of the most popular areas of paddlesport. Like the Inuit hunter, an expert ocean kayaker can be more or less invincible. In addition to the paddling techniques and skills, you will need to acquire the knowledge to be a wily mariner and look after yourself at sea.

BITCHES FOG STORY

The Bitches tidal rapid is a strange place, next to an island a mile offshore from mainland Britain. It has been a Mecca for playboaters for many years, but it's in the middle of the sea. Sea kayakers are often very au fait with the skills to get there and back, but are challenged by the sheer speed of current and size of standing waves, hydraulics and whirlpools that they aren't used to finding in a marine environment. Whitewater paddlers are good at this, but aren't quite ready for the navigation, the tidal changes and the long transits that are required to manage a trip by sea.

Jason, Steve and I were experienced kayakers, all members of the GB Freestyle Team. We'd travelled to the Bitches to train in big water conditions. We'd been there before, so we knew what to do. The long ferry glide/transit out to the rapid didn't faze us, and we knew what to expect from the paddle home – 15 minutes of hard slog through giant waves and haystacks, followed by a high-pressure transit across a brutally fast current that funnels the unwary kayaker straight into lethal Horse Rock rapid. Not scary for us. We'd done it many times.

So, because we weren't 'sea kayaking' we had all the safety equipment necessary for a park and play mission. None, in other words. It was a sunny day, we had the right clothing on should it turn chilly, and there were three of us. We felt safe – when joined by a couple more paddlers, even safer. We showed off our freestyle skills with impunity. All the while wondering what that strange, booming sound could be.

It was a fog horn. I looked upstream and the 20km of blue sky visibility to the horizon had shrunk to 200m, to a wall of grey mist. 'Guys,' I said, 'we have to go.'

We paddled out to the edge of the rapid, as we always did. The visibility was severely compromised. I could just see a headland on the far shore, and I could see the sun behind me through the fog. 'Last chance, guys... do we go, or wait on the island for the fog to clear?' We all knew that could be tomorrow. No food, no sleeping bags, no dry clothes. Someone asked if I reckoned we could make it. I said I thought yes, if we went now, paddled hard, and were a bit lucky. Unanimous response. We go.

As I peeled out of that last eddy, I still didn't think it was too crazy. But after about one minute I couldn't see the rocks we'd left, and I couldn't see the mainland. All I could see was the next paddler in line behind me, the glimmer of the sun in the sky, and the water I was paddling on. Luckily the strange crisscross waves in the first section of the transit give a very good clue about which way the current was going. I called back for everyone to keep the man behind them in sight. I heard some muffled shouts. Sound travels a long way over water in the fog. I got my head down and sprinted like I never had before.

Suddenly, the water changes from choppy to dead calm. This is where Bitches newbies ease off, but in fact it's the dangerous part, a tongue of current racing at 25 knots directly to Horse Rock. It's impossible to ferry glide – you just have to paddle straight for the mainland. Which I couldn't see. My only hope was the sun behind me. Which I couldn't see. I just hoped I hadn't turned too much as I entered the current. I could be sprinting straight downstream to certain death. Or upstream, same effect, eventually. Dammit. Mind racing. Waiting to see the Horse's curling front wave emerge from the mist, hoping I could still dodge one side or the other. Or perhaps we were hopelessly lost, being washed out into the Irish Sea. Stupid kayakers. Just keep paddling the direction you think you were paddling in. Nothing else matters.

The water feels different, under the hull, a slight swirling of a deep eddy fence. I can see something looming above me. I'm 20m from the cliffs of the mainland, and I've hit the eddy higher than ever before. Adrenalin and blind luck. The others emerge from the mist one by one behind me. Tightest grouping I ever saw on that transit too. Five relieved but very sheepish boaters hit the bar that night. There were a lot of things we should have taken – strobe light, VHF radio, spare paddles, towlines, bivvy bags. Just a simple compass would have made it easy.

◄↓ **The strange tidal currents of the infamous Bitches rapid. A Mecca for sea kayakers and playboaters alike, but very much not to be taken lightly.**

WIND, WAVES, TIDES AND CURRENTS

When you go paddling on open water, wind, waves and distance are your main challenges. Understanding the first two is a big advantage in conquering the third. Use the conditions to your advantage, and you can at least double your pace or range.

WIND

It doesn't take a lot of wind to affect a kayak. Most of the boat is up above the surface of the water and only a little bit below. Intuitively one might think that paddling into the wind (called a headwind, or 'paddling upwind') would be the major obstacle to progress, but while that does slow down the paddler, crosswind and following wind is equally as difficult, and much more frustrating too!

Many paddlers enjoy fast downwind runs in a kayak, but you constantly have to contend with a phenomenon called 'weathercocking'. All kayaks have a tendency to turn back towards the wind. It's tiring and annoying because you're spending more energy doing correcting strokes to keep the boat straight than actually paddling forwards for speed. Going directly downwind, it gets on the nerves that you never know which way the boat will veer next! A well-designed sea kayak with upturned ends and a drop-down skeg may deal with it so well that it's not a big problem, but most lesser craft will suffer. In particular, in a kayak that doesn't have good directional stability – like a GP or whitewater kayak – even a slight breeze can be really tedious.

Weathercocking is also an issue when you have to paddle with the wind coming from one side or the other (crosswind), but at least you know which way the boat is trying to turn. You can respond to this by edging or leaning, or doing a wider, sweepier stroke on the windward side. If you have a rudder, you can offset it slightly towards the wind to compensate for the effect.

When planning your adventure, consult weather forecasts rather than just judging the wind as it appears at the time. Shipping forecast websites and apps are available and much better than information

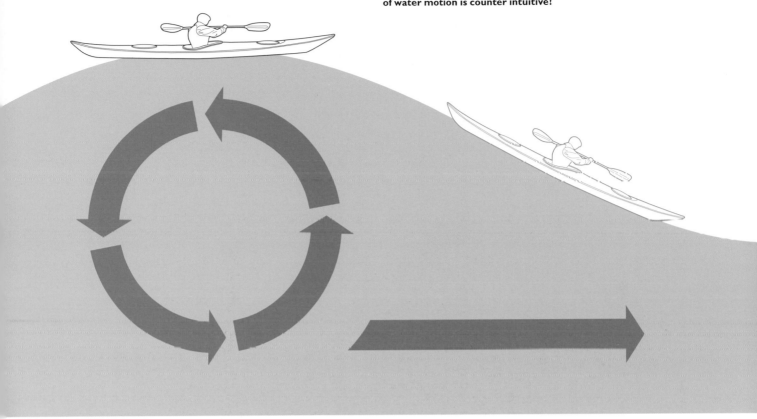

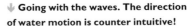
**Going with the waves. The direction
of water motion is counter intuitive!**

about the wind expected on land. Remember that the wind can switch around quite drastically. In warm weather the land cools overnight but the water holds its temperature, so convection currents drive the wind offshore. As the land temperature rises during the day, the wind slowly reverses to blow onshore, as the air that's been warmed by the land rises and sucks cooler air in from over the water. Seafaring folk refer to a wind blowing onshore as 'on a lee shore'. An offshore wind gives us a 'weather shore'. There are lots of terms to remember if you're going to ask salty old seadogs for weather advice.

WAVES

In open water, waves are caused by the friction of the wind on the surface. The only exception is when the water is moving swiftly across shallow rocks or a reef or through a narrow gap. In these moving water examples, though, the effect is exactly the same as it would be in a rapid, and we can bring river skills to bear on the situation.

Back to the wind-waves situation. Although it often appears otherwise, the water isn't actually moving across the surface. It's moving up and down in a slightly circular motion, as shown. The wave energy is moving along, and all kinds of clever things are happening that we don't need to know about. But know this:

GOING WITH THE WAVES

It's hard to paddle up the back of a wave, because you're going uphill, but also because the wave rotation is slightly opposing you. It's easy to paddle down the front of a wave because you're going downhill (you may even start surfing), but the rotation is still against you. If you can get the boat moving quickly while it's still low down on the wave, it'll be easy to keep it moving for a long time. So put all your power into it there, and then you can rest for a bit. This seems to be the most efficient way.

Unless the wave is approaching a surf-beach type situation, you can't stay on the front of the wave all the way to your destination. This is because of some physics. In open water the wave energy is actually travelling faster than the wave, so as you get an assisted ride on the face of a wave, the wave in front of you is growing and the wave you're on is shrinking, and eventually you won't be able to stay on it. So just take the free ride, and then try to keep the boat moving gently as you sink down the back, until you can sprint for another wave as it starts to lift your tail.

GOING AGAINST THE WAVES

I wish I could say that I have a cunning strategy for paddling head-on at the waves, but I don't. Kayaking into oncoming waves, it seems best just to maintain a constant pace as you would on flat water. If the waves are very steep you may get a little surf down the back, but not enough to be worth breaking your rhythm for.

CHOP

Random little waves, made by gusting winds over short distances, are known as chop. These waves just seem like pyramids of water jumping up and down all around you, but you can still take the free ride described above. The main problem is that you can get bogged down with both ends of your kayak buried in two different waves. Try not to fight it. Just relax and trust your balance. If you need to make a change of direction, make it when the middle of the boat is on top of a wave and the end's in free air. This will be the quickest, easiest turn you ever made.

A calm sea can become choppy in a matter of seconds if the wind gusts or changes. Yet the waves often seem to come at you from all directions. Just ignore them and concentrate on your pace and direction.

➜ **Get ready to turn the boat as it gets to the tipping point at the top of the wave.**

SWELL

Swells are the big rolling waves that sweep across the ocean from their origins in big storms far away, and eventually crash on our shores as surf. The longer and stronger the wind has been blowing at their source, the bigger the swells will be when they finally escape the clutches of the wind. The really counter-intuitive thing is that they don't seem to shrink again once they start their trans-oceanic journey – not until they reach the drag of the seabed as the waters get shallower again, unless they're faced with strong winds in the opposite direction.

Because of the way they're made, swells are big in large oceans but less so in small enclosed seas like the Mediterranean. However, they can occur anywhere, and waves of up to 2m (6ft) are common even in some of the larger lakes of the world. But there's another factor that considerably affects the range and power of waves, and that's their wavelength or period.

The further that a (say) 2m swell has been driven across the water (this distance is called its 'fetch'), the longer its gap to the next wave will be. Now, perhaps you can visualise that a wave that's 200m (220yd) 'thick' with a 2m maximum height carries a lot more raised water (and hence wave energy) than a 2m wave that's only 100m (110yd) thick. About 70% more, I guess. This makes a particular difference to the power the wave can deliver when it breaks on a reef or beach. Surf reports often give a wave period in seconds – this is the time between peaks in deep water. However, because waves all travel at about the same speed, the period pretty much tells you whether it's a thick wave or not. Eight seconds is quite a short period, sixteen seconds a very long one.

CHOPPY SWELL

Don't forget that chop can be superimposed on swells if it's windy where you are. This isn't too confusing, but can be quite intimidating. Try to ignore the chop and focus on the swells. It can make it hard to make any use of the swell energy, though, if you're constantly caught up in chop.

WIND WITH OR AGAINST THE WAVES

If the wind is blowing with the waves, it has the effect of flattening out the whole shooting match, at least a little. The waves or chop will be less steep and less pointy. However, wind against waves gives us steep, even vertical faces with long sloping backs. At the shore, an onshore wind gives us crumbly breaking wave faces and a lot of white water, whereas an offshore wind makes steep, peeling faces and 'spindrift', water blowing off the top of the wave.

TIDES

Everywhere there's water, there are tides. In some parts of the world they're small, high water being only a few inches or centimetres above low water. At the other extreme are places of huge tidal range. The Bay of Fundy in Nova Scotia has the greatest mean spring range with 14.5m (47.5ft), and a total recorded range of 16.3m (53.5ft). Other places of comparable range are Ungava Bay in northern Quebec, King Sound in Western Australia, the Gulf of Khambhat in India, and of course the Severn Estuary in the UK.

Although high and low tides are caused by the gravitational pull of

TIDAL FLOW

Tidal flow is a very complex thing to understand, but it's important to know what the tide's going to do where you're paddling. It's not just a case of the sea rising and falling. The huge amounts of water in motion cause strong currents in many areas, especially areas of large tidal range, or narrow estuaries. There could also be tidal waves called 'bores', like the famous one on the Severn Estuary in the UK and the Yangtze Estuary in China. There can even be huge rapids formed by the flow of the tide over rocks and ledges, like the one at the Bitches in Wales, or another at Skookumchuck Narrows in British Columbia, Canada.

OCEAN WAVES

You've read all about being careful in the surf, and whatever kind of boat you paddle, the surf kayaking section may come in handy too. It's important that you don't underestimate the immense power of breaking waves. Once you're in deep, open water, however, waves don't tend to break with crushing force, and when they do break it's a transient thing that lets go of you pretty quickly.

OVERFALLS

Overfalls happen in the sea, but not usually in a river. They're usually caused by swells, but sometimes by big tidal changes. The word describes what happens when water pours over a rock, forming a pourover-like feature, but also surging through gaps and over ledges like a small waterfall. They're fun to play in if you're confident, but they're constantly changing and there's a lot of scope for boat or skin damage, as you can be unceremoniously dumped on to rocks as the overfalls surge.

the moon, they're also affected by the sun. That's why high tides aren't all the same height – when sun and moon work together we have spring tides, which are the most extreme highs and lows. At the other end of the scale are neap tides, with not very high tides but equally moderate low tides. Spring tides have nothing to do with the seasons, by the way. They occur every two weeks, with neaps the intervening week, in a constant weekly cycle of undulating tidal range. Get yourself a tide table or a tide app for your phone or computer, and it's easy to keep track of the tides wherever you are.

NAVIGATION

Even if the sea or lake is calm, it's easy to get into some bother if you can't orientate yourself over long distances, and perhaps without clear landmarks to aim for. Luckily, recent technology has made it very easy to do this without special skills or training, as long as you understand a few basic principles.

GPS VERSUS CELLPHONE

You can buy a lot of different navigation devices that use global positioning satellites (GPS) to give an exact position. The most basic ones require you to translate that information into a position on a paper map or chart. Some come with preloaded maps that can help to make the job a lot simpler. However, for kayakers who are rarely more than 3km (2 miles) from land, it's unusual to be out of range of a cellphone signal. A modern cellphone equipped with GPS can use Google Maps or similar, obtained live from the Internet, to help you with your route and positioning. Many GPS units and some cellphones are waterproof already, but if not it's fairly easy to acquire a waterproof case. I often just use a ziplock bag. It's a bit fragile, but if you put it away somewhere careful when you're not using it, you can preserve it well enough to keep your device dry and still be able to use the buttons.

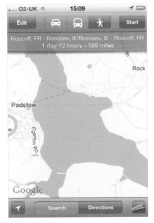

Because technology can have its glitches, and batteries often run flat or are subject to human error, I'd always back up the navigation system with a compass and map if the undertaking is in any way hazardous. Many sea kayaks come with a spherical compass mounting on the deck. This is better than the flatter compasses used on land, because the latter only work properly when held level!

← A cellphone or a standalone GPS can be invaluable to the sea kayaker, and each have their unique advantages.

↑ Maps can be laminated to make them waterproof, and some sprayskirts have a system to hold a map in place close enough to check it easily.

If you don't have a compass, you can orientate yourself by day using an analogue watch and the sun. Point the hour hand at the horizon directly below where the sun is. Halfway between that direction and 12 o'clock in an anticlockwise direction is south – if you're in the Northern Hemisphere. In the Southern Hemisphere it indicates north. If you're on or near the Equator I guess this is going to be confusing. But it's still clever, huh?

At night this system doesn't work, but over short time-periods you can consider the constellation where the sun went down, if the sky is clear. If you know a bit more about stargazing, you may be able to navigate well by the stars, as more ancient mariners did. And sometimes at night it's even easier to spot things on the land than it is by day, because of the onshore lights. Even so, I'd still want a compass. The sky isn't always clear, nor the visibility good.

TRANSITS

You don't need any training to use basic navigational tools on open water journeys. A willingness to use common sense and think outside the box is pretty valuable. But one thing you really need to understand is the concept of a transit. If you understand how to ferry glide in a current (see page 126) it may be easier to adapt your paddling to the conditions. But the basic principle is this:

Let's say you are going from A to B, and it's a straight line on the map if you use one, or on the water anyway. But there's a current, or a wind that isn't directly with or against you. Well, you're going to have to make allowance for that. You can point your boat directly at the destination, if you can see it, or on a compass bearing, but as you paddle you'll drift off course, and if you keep adjusting it to point at the destination you'll have paddled in a big arc. It's often better to set a course that's angled to compensate for the 'drift' from the outset. A bit like a ferry glide.

To do this takes experience of how fast and far the wind and/or current will carry you. With a GPS, however, you can program your journey in and see your position drifting off-line as you paddle. You can then adjust your angle upwind or upcurrent to try to stay on the desired line. You're still paddling further than the distance appears as the seagull flies, but you're staying on track and in control of your destiny.

Don't try to transit or ferry glide if the wind/current is stronger than you are. In this instance it's better to sprint straight across, accepting that you'll get carried off-line, but dramatically reducing your time exposed to the problem. See the Bitches story at the start of this chapter!

DISTANCE AND PACE

One of the advantages of a GPS, whether dedicated or part of your cellphone, is that it can usually tell you how far you travel and at what speed. This is invaluable for keeping track of your journey, and informative for planning future ones. Don't place 100% faith in the readings, though. Make sure you've thought about wind and current – because the GPS measures ground speed, not water speed.

To give you an idea, a fast touring or sea kayak can be comfortably paddled at about five knots (nautical term). A knot (kt) is one nautical mile per hour, and it's a bit faster than mph in your car: 1 knot = 1.15mph or 1.85kph. Approximately.

If you sprint you might manage 7kt (nearly 13kph) but you can't keep that up. In fact even five is unlikely to be a sustainable pace all day. And you need to stop for meals and other calls of nature.

Double sea kayaks are not that common, but they are a great way for two people to enjoy the ocean together. They are fast, and have some advantages if one paddler is less confident.

So experience has shown that 25 miles per day is a reasonable expectation of distance covered, day in and day out.

It's important to know the limits of your endurance. How far can the weakest person in the party paddle? And how fast? Ask yourself at the planning stage, not when things get complicated. Bear in mind that your range on calm and sheltered water may be very different from that which you can manage in wind and waves. Experience counts here.

Children, and some adults for that matter, run out of energy very quickly, and when that happens they often refuse to co-operate. Or paddle. This is where your towing skills may well be called upon. Being in a double kayak with someone who can carry them as a passenger is another solution.

CLOTHING

→ **Sea kayak shell.**

→ **A modern touring or sea kayaking buoyancy aid with ample pockets.**

→ **Despite lacking some of the features of a whitewater dry top, the sea kayaking shell is quite suitable for some pretty rough conditions.**

↓ **Setting out to sea, well equipped with a sea kayaking shell, hood zipped away in the collar, and a good-quality touring buoyancy aid.**

Many kayakers use the same apparel for different kayaking disciplines rather than own lots of sets of kit. Thermals, fleece clothing and other insulation is, of course, applicable anywhere. But open-water touring kayakers tend to eschew neoprene wetsuit garments, partly because there's little need for it – impact protection in shallow water isn't the sea kayaker's prime concern – but also because wearing neoprene for long periods can become uncomfortable, especially in a salt environment. Waterproof shell garments worn over thermals are likely to be the touring paddler's preferred clothing choice.

While many boaters do choose a dry top just like that worn by the whitewater paddler, a touring paddler is more likely to consider ventilation. Adjustable opening necks are a good idea, perhaps combined with a hood in case the weather gets really bad. But if the weather is more clement, paddling in just a shirt or a basic windproof top can be a lot more pleasant. I notice that most people seem to overdress for the conditions, rather than carrying extra clothes for emergencies. But you have a big boat full of storage space, so use it!

SAFETY, RESCUE SKILLS AND EQUIPMENT

One of the most important safety precautions you can take is some kind of lighting, in case you don't make it ashore before nightfall. A head-torch is a very useful thing for finding stuff in the back of your boat, but it's not great for paddling. You'll just light up the deck and ruin everyone's night vision. It's better to have a light on your back so that others can see you, but you can let your own eyes get accustomed to the dark.

FLARES

If you're going offshore, it's a good idea to carry one or more rescue flares and to know how to use them. They're still the best way to show your location to would-be rescuers. Most sea kayaking buoyancy aids have a back pocket that's designed to accommodate the most common type of flares.

RE-ENTRY METHODS

It's perfectly possible to get back into your boat on your own, if the sea is reasonably calm and your boat and paddle aren't being tossed around. Just slither up on to the back deck and, taking care to keep your balance, get into the seat. Practice is key, though, or you won't manage well when you need to. Because sea kayaks have watertight compartments, there won't be much water in the cockpit once you get in and displace it, and this can be pumped out with a hand pump, or baled out with anything to hand. Even your hat!

As we've seen elsewhere, the paddle can be secured under the decklines of the boat to stop it from drifting away, but also to act as a bit of a stabiliser. Some paddlers use a 'paddle float', an inflatable device like a child's water wings. This is inflated around the paddle blade and turns the paddle into a sort of outrigger, making it much easier to get on to an unstable sea kayak from the water. If you don't want to buy a special float, this works just as well using a spare buoyancy aid.

→ This paddler is wearing a high-intensity strobe light. It can be used as a torch, but also to help the rescue services find you in the water.

→ The chemical lightstick is a cheap safety light to make you more visible at night. It's single use only, but lasts for several hours.

⬇ A paddle-float ready for action on the back deck of a touring kayak.

← With a simple loop of webbing or a climbing sling, you can tow a kayak for short distances, and it's really easy to disengage if you need to. I prefer to leave it around my arm or elbow. It feels a little awkward, but it's safer than putting it over your head!

TOWING

Where long distances are concerned, one of the most important skills, after self-recovery and basic boat-to-boat rescues, is the ability to drag someone out of a difficult corner or tow them for a significant distance if they're unable to paddle. Sometimes it's a handy skill just to get an empty boat from one place to another.

There are many different commercial towing systems available, but a lot of paddlers make their own. The most important thing with any tow is that it's easily releasable in the event of anything getting complicated. Most commercial towlines have a quick-release for the tower to dump the tow, but many systems overlook the need for the towee to be able to disengage too.

It's pretty common to tow from the waist, but a lot of sea paddlers use a deck-mounted system. Sea kayaks can be very heavy, so it's good for this load not to be jerking at your lower back. The most common system is to capture the tow-rope in a 'jam cleat' bolted to the back deck. It can be quick-released simply by pulling the rope upwards out of the cleat.

However, I find that towing from behind is problematic. We're rarely called upon to tow someone in ideal conditions. Usually wind and waves are tossing the boats around. When the tow is behind, you can't see the rope to know whether it's slack or tight, or when it's going to be. The towed boat could be surfing towards you and about to hit you in the back of the head! So I've adopted a tow from the bow.

My quick-release is made from a whitewater chest belt release system and a Velcro retainer copied from surfboard leashes. This

holds a webbing towline that runs through the bow loop and back to me. The tow hook is attached to the decklines where I can reach it. I can use this as a close tow, or let out some more webbing to a short tow, or attach another rope to make a long tow. But

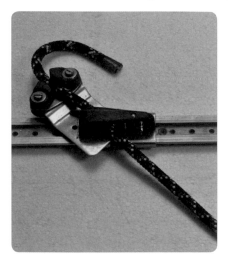

← A common jam cleat quick-release.

→ The components of most towing systems: a shock absorber, a rope adjusted using a 'daisy chain' method, a metal hook, and a float to stop the hook from sinking. Hooks for use in the sea should be stainless steel.

➜ Here's a short tow using my bow tow system. This method works equally well for any length of tow, since it's adjustable on the deck in front of the paddler.

➜ Sometimes it's best to be a long way away from the other kayak, or sometimes there isn't any choice. This is a long tow using a throwline, and pulling from the waist this time.

most importantly, it can be used to tow my boat. If someone throws me a line, I can clip on to it myself and it's attached to the bow, to tow or be towed. And this system can be quick-released by the person being towed.

THROW TOW

The throw tow is a simple matter of using a river-style throwline as the tow rope. This can be thrown to the victim by the rescuer or vice versa. It can be carried attached to the decklines of the boat, or around the waist using a utility belt which can double as a tow belt. The throwline can be daisy-chained to make it shorter and/or act as a shock absorber.

➜ This utility belt allows quick access to a throwline, as well as attachment points for towing and carrying other bits of kit.

CHAPTER 6

KAYAKING COMPETITION

Kayaking has a wide diversity of competitive disciplines, from the thrills and spills of whitewater to the sheer athletic focus of Olympic sprint racing. What follows is an overview of a few styles of competition to give you a feel for them...

Maybe you don't need this section of the book. If you just want to go kayaking, and have no further ambition than that, then you don't. But you've picked the book up and read it a bit, so I'm guessing there's at least a part of you that's already a little in love with kayaking and wants to be more awesome at it.

When I first started to compete and paddle difficult or dangerous water, I had no idea about training, or sport psychology, and neither did most of the people around me. What I realised over a period of time was that the more that I was able to mimic the thoughts and actions of the top guys, the more I was able to produce similar results. Even the paddlers who just seem ridiculously talented and never train, nor worry about their nutrition, still seem to have something to offer if you look at their mental attitude and habits.

In this chapter I mention video a lot. It's entirely my own subjective opinion now, but I think it's a waste of time and money to watch countless commercial videos about kayaking. Sure, it's inspiring – it was seeing the world's best boaters on the TV screen that motivated me to take up kayaking in the first place. And I still watch them sometimes. Or at least, the teaser trailer or the edited highlights. But when you're trying to improve your skills, it's all about *achievable* goals. So it would

be better to spend time watching yourself on video, or people who are better than you but not out of reach.

Time and money spent watching the best of the best seems to me flawed in two respects. First, it's time and money that could have been spent on paddling, or training. Second, a commercial video doesn't show the athletes' everyday paddling. It shows their best-ever paddling. Which is pretty misleading as a goal. I've trained a lot of people who said, 'I can do X'. And I'd say, 'Can you do it now, when I say go? Or can you just do it sometimes?' And that, fundamentally, is the difference. Eventually even the best work from the best of the best won't be out of reach.

The best way for you to move your paddling forward is to learn how to become an expert at goal-setting and mimicry. If you set achievable yet challenging goals in each of the areas you want to improve, you'll be well on your way. Learn to imitate great achievers and you'll learn the fast-track route to conquering your goals and becoming a champion. Although I can't spend much time on goal-setting here, let me suggest that you be as specific as possible about it. Write your goals down, and use an inspiring photo and a quotation that'll help you to feel like a champion every time you see them!

The best way to mimic someone whose performance you admire is to watch them on video. In real life we're always a little bit too slow to pick up on what's important. Take a video camera with you and record everything. Then watch it back, and concentrate not on what paddlers achieved, but what they actually did to make that happen. That's what you need to imitate.

I've outlined a training schedule that helps me. I use it for kayaking as well as other sports like skiing that have different seasons. My year of any given sport is split up into three seasons, the off-season, the pre-season and the in-season.

OFF-SEASON TRAINING

The off-season training begins when the paddling season ends, and is a minimum of two to three months in which I try to recover mentally and physically. Depending on the area in which you live, this period could be longer – maybe you're snowed in all winter! During this time I try to stay active in any way other than paddling. I try to concentrate on activities that'll improve my performance the following season.

This off-season period should include an aerobic and anaerobic training programme. Bicycling, swimming, weight training, or cross-country skiing are all excellent activities that will keep your body developing for the upcoming season. In the past I never used to train at the gym, but now I'm convinced of the benefits of a weight-training programme that's designed by a professional strength and conditioning coach to suit my goals and the season that I'm in. The name of the game is to improve your strength and fitness while not over-taxing the bits on which the paddling season has taken a heavy toll.

Although I'm not paddling in the off-season, I'll still be a kayaker in my head. Watching videos, reading books, and keeping in touch with the paddling world online all help to keep mind and body focused, so that when you come to paddling again you'll bring something more to the table.

PRE-SEASON TRAINING

After several months of not kayaking, I'm stronger, healthier and more enthusiastic about paddling again. The main aim now is to ramp up performance in the boat from your current ability to the maximum that can reasonably be expected through the in-season. This means concentrating on making sure the basic stuff you can already do is as perfect as it can be, to form the best possible foundation for improving the more difficult skills. These can then be alternated in practice sessions – easy stuff, difficult stuff, with the harder stuff getting the bar raised every time, according to your pre-determined goals. You'll need to sit down every couple of weeks and revise your goals, because you may have set them too high, or too low, and you'll only ever know by comparing progress to goals.

At this point I'm still cross-training and training at the gym as well as skills training in the boat. Posture, stability and strength all need to be managed throughout, so that when you arrive at the season proper, you're in optimal condition to paddle to your maximum output level up to five times a week.

By training progressively, your condition increases at the same rate as the difficulty of your performance. Of course, it depends whether you're training for long distance or a 60-second freestyle performance, but whatever it is, work up to it slowly through this period. I find that this is the hardest discipline challenge I face. I love kayaking, so it's hard for me to do it for just half an hour, at less than maximal output, and then just go home.

When focusing on your training programme don't forget to concentrate on the basics, like warming up and cooling down, and stretching. These are easily overlooked in this build-up phase.

IN-SEASON TRAINING

In a perfect world, at this stage I'll be paddling five consecutive days a week, under performance conditions and with a focused mindset. Video analysis of my paddling continues to allow me to iron out any little kinks in the performance. It takes a lot of willpower to take two full days off, but the recovery time is essential if you aren't to become over-tired or even ill.

If the goal is speed, train over race distance. If the goal is a slalom run, do full-length runs. Practise your actual freestyle routine three times back to back and then go and watch it on video, and try again when you're completely recovered. Because that's what happens in a competition. Every discipline is different, but it's very important to practise exactly what you hope to perform. Not twice as much at half the effort, or vice versa!

If you try putting your calendar under this kind of scrutiny, I think you'll be able to accomplish much more than you ever have before. But please be sensible and remember to keep your paddling in perspective – don't neglect other important areas of your life. Remember, it's just for fun!

SLALOM

Slalom is one of kayaking's Olympic disciplines, and while the kayaks haven't changed very much for several decades, the spectacle of high-performance boats racing over a tricky and technical course on powerful white water is, if anything, more awesome than ever.

The sport is a time trial, with one person or team on the rapid at a time, and the paddlers have to negotiate a series of gates formed by poles hanging over the rapids. The green and white gates must be taken downstream, and the red and white in an upstream direction. The paddler must pass through the gate without touching either of the poles. A gate judge will be watching closely to detect the slightest contact. If you hit a pole, a penalty will be added to your overall time. Miss a gate completely and you incur a bigger penalty that probably renders the time uncompetitive. So there's no tactical missing of gates. It's usually worth coming back for a second attempt at the gate, so punitive is the time penalty for a complete fail.

Each competitor will usually have one or more practice runs once the course has been set out, and then there'll be two timed runs, the better of which counts to determine the overall ranking. Competitors study the course in great detail, planning every paddle stroke in their quest for the quickest line through all the gates. The fitness and power of the top competitors is impressive, their whitewater paddling skills

perhaps even more so. They really make a difficult rapid look easy as they use the water to help them from gate to gate.

There are a number of different categories in a slalom competition. The kayak classes are men's and women's kayak, both paddling the same type of boat, which will be 3.5m (12ft) in length and at least 60cm (2ft) in width. There's also sometimes a team event in which a group of three paddlers negotiate the course together. The collective time is taken as that from the first paddler to cross the start line, to the final paddler crossing the finish. All three paddlers must finish within a 15-second window, and all of their individual penalties are added on. It's a pretty exciting race!

Slalom kayaks are usually made from carbon fibre, or Kevlar, or a combination of the two. They're so lightweight you could probably lift one with one finger. They're quite fragile for paddling rapids with abrasive rocks all over the place, but slalom paddlers are skilful. And careful.

Slalom used to be the natural choice in whitewater paddling, and the way that most people honed their paddling skills, but sadly most people start in plastic kayaks now, and are less likely to become really precise, because the short and more forgiving boats allow them to bounce down rapids with a lesser degree of control. This isn't to denigrate the skills of top-level whitewater paddlers – slalom has

been described as grade 5 moves with grade 3 consequences – it's just that entering the sport in GP boats has meant that fewer and fewer paddlers are taking it up.

Slalom has been a part of the Olympic Games since its inclusion in 1972, and continues to be wherever the host country can create a reliable whitewater rapid. These are usually artificial whitewater courses made from concrete and plastic, which go on to be an enduring resource for whitewater boaters in that country for many years to come. The 1972 Olympic course, called the Eiskanal, in

Augsburg, Germany, is still very popular to this day. Slalom's inclusion in the London 2012 Olympics has no doubt captured a lot of paddlers' imaginations, so I look forward to seeing a lot more 'stick-chasing' action in the future.

As an aside, I should mention that slalom isn't only about kayaking. Slalom canoes look very similar to the kayaks, but are paddled kneeling and with a single bladed paddle, and they're an awesome spectacle. There are single and double classes of canoe called C1 and C2, and they're both included in the Olympics too.

⬆⬇ **Slalom paddlers are characterised by this high stroke style with a fusion of power strokes, rudders and draws. Of course not hitting the poles with the paddle is as important as the body or the boat.**

➜ **Slalomists talk a lot about keeping the deck dry – going over waves not through them, and keeping the hull planing wherever possible, is the key to going faster.**

Within the governing bodies of the International Canoe Federation, which covers both canoeing and kayaking (hence the name), there has usually been a whitewater racing discipline as well as a slalom one. This is usually performed in long, high-volume kayaks, less manoeuvrable than slalom kayaks but much faster in a straight line. Races are usually held over 500m (550yd) or so, and there are no gates to negotiate – it's just about who's quickest from the start line to the finish. Like slalom, there's usually a K1 men's and women's category, as well as a C1 and C2 class.

With the advent of high-performance creek boats, a lot of whitewater boaters began to paddle rapids that are just too technical for the old-fashioned whitewater racer. This led to the sport of extreme racing, wherein kayakers would race against the clock on really hard rapids, usually grade 5. This is still popular with many paddlers, but the up and coming racing discipline is the sport of boatercross. Two, three or four paddlers race at the same time over a difficult section of water, usually grade 3–4, and this means that they're vying with each other for the best line down the rapid. Which of course makes it even more exciting. It's not for the faint-hearted, and there are a lot of clashes and wipeouts. You need to be right on top of your game on rapids of this level, to even think about racing down them with other people trying to get in your way. But it is an amazing sport to watch.

⬇ **Fun racing on the artificial whitewater course in Cardiff, Wales, UK. This rapid is grade 3 only, but at the highest level expert paddlers are racing down class 5+ and waterfalls!**

FREESTYLE

Freestyle kayaking competition is an ever-changing discipline, as new moves are invented all the time and the top whitewater paddlers are constantly pushing the limits of what's possible. Therefore even if you bought a book specifically focused on freestyle, it would date very quickly. What doesn't change much is the nature of freestyle – that it's about fun rather than adrenalin; that it may have rules, and a stopwatch, but that it's all about inventiveness and how good the moves look. Hence the name freestyle.

It wasn't always called that. Paddlers in various parts of the world remember this differently, but my recollection is that it all started with slalom kayakers performing tricks on waves or in holes, and that some people called that 'hot-dogging' – a term that I think was borrowed from skiing, though skiers too call it freestyle these days. Anyway, as shorter plastic boats came along in the 1970s and '80s, hot-dogging became more and more popular, and people started to arrange increasingly organised freestyle get togethers, which somehow became commonly known as 'rodeo' competitions. They were based on a common practice: a group of paddlers would wait in an eddy as each one took a turn to attempt the best trick or series of tricks on a wave or hole. The game was judged completely subjectively, with the competitors often simply voting amongst themselves on the best rides.

In the late 20th century the sport was more popular in many countries than the other, older whitewater competitions, and the rules and judging became more rigid and formal. A panel of judges would allocate points to each move from a list, as each competitor took a ride of a limited time, usually 45 seconds or so. It made it difficult to invent moves, as anything new wouldn't necessarily score points if it wasn't on the list, and led to a focus on 'combination moves' following quickly in sequence with no break. At the time of writing the emphasis seems to be on aerial moves performed completely above the water, but this depends very much on the type of wave that the competition is being held on.

Freestyle probably isn't the biggest whitewater competition discipline now, the main reason being that the boats have become so extremely specialised that they wouldn't be anyone's choice of river-running kayak any more. Most paddlers only want one kayak, so that's freestyle out of the window – if they get involved in competition it's more likely to be river racing or boatercross.

One of the lovely things about freestyle is that so many of those paddlers who don't really want to compete in a formal structure still have these little gatherings and vie with each other to see who can do the best tricks. Many of these people aren't even paddling playboats, but are attempting tricks in their creek boat, crossover boat, GP boat or whatever they happen to be paddling. Which takes us right back to where the sport began. Rather a nice thing, I think.

→ **The loop is currently the trademark move in freestyle kayaking.**

⇓ **James "Pringle" Bebbington and the kind of aerial move that made him 2011 World Champion.**

KAYAK SPRINT AND MARATHON

↑ **James Keeble racing in the Nottingham Sprints, 2011.**

Sprint and marathon are the flatwater racing disciplines of the kayak world. Using broadly similar racing kayaks that are extremely light, very unstable and, of course, lightning quick, the athletes who practise this kind of paddling are some of the fittest and most powerful you'll ever see in a kayak.

Sprint is an Olympic discipline, first featured as a demonstration sport at the Paris 1924 Games. It became a full Olympic sport in 1936, when races were held over distances of 1,000m and 10,000m. Since then, the Olympic events have been shortened, with the 10,000m events last being held at the Melbourne 1956 Games. Today the athletes race over 200, 500 or 1,000m.

In kayaks, athletes race either single (men's K1 and women's K1), in pairs (men's K2 and women's K2), or in fours (men's K4 and women's K4). It should be mentioned that there are very similar C1, C2 and C4 events for canoes, paddled with a single-bladed paddle and a high, drop knee, kneeling position. The races are usually held on sheltered inland boating lakes, many of them built for the purpose of racing canoes, kayaks and rowing boats.

The format of the competition depends on how many boats are competing. In events with ten boats, the competition starts with two heats. The winner of each heat goes straight into the final, with the rest going forward to one semi-final. The best six boats from the semi-final progress to the final.

Events with 11 to 16 boats start with two heats and it gets a bit more complicated! If there are 11 to 12 boats competing, the winning boat from each heat progresses straight to the A final, with the other boats going forward to the semi-finals. The top three boats from each

semi-final progress to the A final, while the others advance to the B final (which ranks boats from nine through to 16).

If there are 13 to 14 boats competing, the first five boats in each heat progress to two semi-finals, while the other boats go to the B final. The top four boats from each semi-final progress to the A final, while the others progress to the B final.

If there are 15 to 16 boats competing, the first six boats in each heat progress to two semi-finals, while the other boats go to the B final. The top four boats from each semi-final progress to the A final, while the others progress to the B final.

Events with 17 to 24 boats start with three heats. The first five boats in each heat plus the boat with the best sixth-placed time progress to two semi-finals, while the other boats are out of the competition. The top four boats from each semi-final progress to the A final, while the others progress to the B final.

Officials usually include a chief judge, timekeepers, aligners, start judges, finish judges, boat control officials and umpires.

Sprint depends on immense fitness, emphasising core and upper-body strength, as well as enormous stamina. Great paddling technique is important too, to ensure getting the maximum out of every stroke.

BREAKING THE RULES

Athletes can be penalised for infringements, such as a repeat of a false start or leaving the middle of their lane. A boat that capsizes before the bow crosses the finish line will also be eliminated from the race.

MARATHON KAYAKING

Marathon races are held on rivers, lakes, canals and estuaries over a wide range of distances, in a wide range of craft, but usually flatwater racing kayaks. The minimum distance is usually about 10km, as any less than this would be approaching the realm of sprint kayaking, but there really is something for everyone. The longest race in the world is the Yukon 1000 at 1,000 miles (1,600km). Some other examples include the Dipole Challenge, 170km (105 miles) non-stop through the night in November, in Lithuania. The Devizes to Westminster Marathon in England each Easter is 125 miles (200km). A couple more to note are the 120-mile (193km) Au Sable River Marathon in Michigan, USA, and the Murray Marathon, 404km (250 miles), down the Murray River in Australia.

It's a very different game from training for sprint. You could be

racing for ten miles, or for one hundred. Nutrition and hydration become very important considerations, but the challenges are quite absorbing. In most cases you'll be getting out of the boat to carry it around obstacles (portaging).

In many countries there are regular fixtures of races over different distances, and suited to all abilities. These together with local and regional races and descent races, held downstream on faster moving water, mean that there are races for all skill levels and ages throughout most of the year.

POLO

Canoe polo is a ball game very similar to water polo. Contrary to its name, it's always played in kayaks, not canoes. That misnomer stems from the outdated, peculiarly British habit of calling all paddle-craft 'canoes'.

It's a crazy game, sometimes appearing quite violent, in that it isn't uncommon for paddlers to be capsized by challenges on the ball, so really good rolling and recovery skills are required. Most polo players will have a reliable hand roll, and be called upon to use it often.

The standard format is two teams of five players, who try to carry or pass a football-sized ball by hand or on the deck of the boat, and throw it into the opposing goal, which is a 1.5m (5ft) wide by 1m (3ft) high net suspended above the water at each end of the 'pitch'. The pitch can be set out any way on any piece of water, but it's often in a swimming pool.

Playing water polo is a really good way of learning excellent boat control skills and rolling, and the mental skill of paddling instinctively, because all your conscious focus is on the ball. This is useful for any kind of paddling, so it's a very popular learning tool for club-level paddlers.

Crash helmets and buoyancy aids are compulsory. The helmets have face cages like the ones used in ice hockey, to protect against the ball or errant paddle blades. The buoyancy aids have additional padding in the sides because of the danger of being struck in the torso by a paddle or a boat. There are rules about the minimum radiuses of paddle edges and the ends of the boats.

Although ramming and other raw aggression isn't allowed, it's a full contact sport, so a good deal of pushing and shoving is inevitable. Since both the hands and the paddle may be used to manipulate the ball and to block shots or passes, there is of course regular firm contact between boats, paddles and heads. It's not unusual to be pushed over by another player while jostling for the ball, although there are regulations about pushing – shoulders and arms only.

In 2010, following the World Championships held in Milan, the International Canoe Federation decided to change the rules of polo to add the so-called '60-second shot clock' rule. A team must attempt a shot at goal within 60 seconds of gaining possession or control of the ball. Failure to do so will result in possession being awarded to the other team. This rule, in combination with the current tactic of playing five on five with no goalkeeper, has pushed up the score-lines and made the game even more fast-paced than ever.

Polo is an explosive, exciting sport with a mixture of sprinting, stopping, turning and accelerating, with regular rolling and hand-rolling as well as difficult ball-handling skills. Playing it will definitely give you a good level of all-round paddling fitness.

Most clubs will have a selection of polo boats and paddles, which means that to start out you don't need any specialist equipment of your own. If you do take one thing, though, make it a nose clip. You can only spend so much time upside down in a swimming pool before you wish you'd worn one!

KAYAK SURFING COMPETITION

Like any sport, kayak surfing has an element of competition. It's always difficult to compare and contrast performances in a freestyle discipline, but just as whitewater freestyle has developed its own set of scoring systems for different tricks performed in a ride, kayak surfers have found a subjective but fairly reliable way of measuring their own performance.

Competitive kayak surfing is modelled very much on the pattern of a board surfing event. Judging any freestyle discipline is an inevitably flawed procedure that separates the 'free' from the 'style', but there is no doubt that the competition criteria are clear, and are a great way to shatter any illusions you may have about how good you are!

Kayak surfing competitions are often fairly small and it isn't uncommon for the events to be judged by the competitors themselves. Those who aren't on the water competing will use a judging rota to judge or write down (scribe) the scores of those who are paddling. Larger or international events usually employ professional judges from the boardsurfing community, thus ensuring that the sport continues to mirror the way other surf events are scored.

Kayak surfing is judged on length and quality of ride. The length of ride depends on how long you can stay in the shoulder/power pocket of any wave, and the quality reflects the difficulty of functional manoeuvres you perform in order to do so. The two things really go hand in hand – it's the more 'critical' rides, keeping the kayak as deep as possible in the power zone, that inevitably demonstrate the most radical moves.

To score highly in a kayak surfing competition, you really need to be good at wave selection. Although you'll usually be judged on all waves, with the best three to count, you can't afford to waste time riding a bad wave when there may be a better one behind it. Or to waste energy paddling out again after a low-scoring wave.

The event might be made up of 20 minute heats, with four or five paddlers in each session. The two highest-scoring paddlers go through to the next round, and so on until a final four. There's sometimes then a head-to-head with just two paddlers. It all depends on the number of competitors.

The kayakers will usually set out from the shore at an allotted time, which might be before the end of the previous heat. Flags or banners on the shore are used to signal the start of the heat, with a green flag showing that judging has begun. This flag will normally not be shown until all the competitors have arrived outside the break line, unless it's clear to the judges that because of conditions or ability this is never going to happen. Five minutes before the end of the heat, a yellow flag may be shown to let the paddlers know. They probably have only one more chance to get a wave at this stage. I'd expect them to be checking a watch, though, and to know to the second how things stand time-wise.

It often surprises new competitors in kayak surfing to learn that you don't (usually) score points in a contest for moves which don't serve a functional purpose in extending or maintaining the ride. The exception is the exit move, usually an aerial. However, the more spectacular the techniques you use to achieve a long ride in the critical part of the wave, the more points you'll score. There are also no points for paddle-out tricks, like kickflips and wavewheels, and no points are scored while riding in the white water. It has to be on the green part of the wave.

The format of kayak surfing competition may well change, but the basic principles will no doubt endure, and continue to be influenced by surfing and wave-ski events. Some events do now include a hot-dogging round, or an expression session, which can be judged in a very similar way to freestyle kayaking – or perhaps not at all, and just for fun.

GLOSSARY

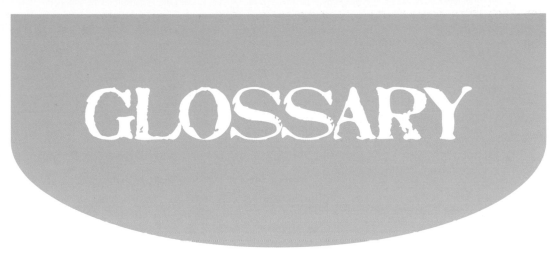

Aerial Any manoeuvre that takes the kayak completely clear of the water, but most commonly heard in freestyle and surfing circles as a trick performed from the face of a wave, and usually with the aim of retaining the wave ride on landing.

Aft Towards the rear of the boat.

Air blade The blade of the paddle that's in the air during a stroke.

Asymmetric A type of paddle with the top edge of the blade longer than the bottom.

Attaining Moving upstream on a rapid by skilfully using eddies.

Backrest (back strap, backband) – A padded fabric device in the kayak to support the lower back and allow the paddler to brace against the footrest.

Beam The width of the boat.

Blade Can mean the bit of the paddle you put in the water, but some people use it as a word for the whole paddle.

Blunt A type of aerial or semi-aerial wave trick that throws the boat end over end after a bounce or aerial.

Boater Generic colloquial term for a kayaker or a canoeist.

Boatercross Kayak race in which two, three or four paddlers race at the same time over a difficult section of water.

Boof A technique for landing the boat flat off a drop, and also the sound it makes.

Bow The front part of the boat.

Bow draw Advanced stroke that pulls the front of the kayak sideways towards the paddle.

Bow rudder Advanced steering stroke at the front of the boat that turns a moving kayak towards the paddle.

Break in To move from an eddy into the current.

Break out To move from the current into an eddy.

Breaking/broken wave When the face of a wave collapses and becomes white water.

Broach When the boat turns sideways.

Buoyancy aid A flotation device, usually worn like a vest. See *PFD*.

Caballito Traditional Peruvian fishing kayak made from reeds.

Cambuckle A type of adjustable buckle that holds a webbing strap by closing a flap or lever.

Capsize To turn upside down in a boat.

Carbon Kevlar A common space-age composite material providing light weight and enormous strength. And cost.

Cartwheel A freestyle trick invented by squirt boaters – the boat somersaults end over end but edge to edge like a gymnastic cartwheel.

Chine Corner or kink in the curvature of the hull.

Choppy/chop Small, pointy waves.

Climbing and dropping Carving up and down while surfing across the face of a wave.

Composite Made from a combination of materials, commonly a resin and a cloth.

Critical (surfing) In the steepest part of the wave close to the breaking 'shoulder'.

Cross bow Any stroke performed with a paddle blade that's usually used on the other side of the boat.

Death eddy A very powerful eddy in a difficult corner that can't be paddled out of easily or has an unsafe exit.

Deck The top side of the kayak; another word for spraydeck or sprayskirt.

Dihedral (paddle) A slightly convex shape on the drive face that stabilises the blade during the stroke.

Displacement The amount of a kayak immersed in the water; a mode of flotation that isn't planing.

Downstream The direction a current flows. Generally towards the sea.

Downwave Towards the bottom/trough of a wave; shoreward side of a wave.

Downwind In the direction the wind is blowing.

Draw stroke Any stroke that moves the boat sideways.

Drop Any significant slope or step down in a current. See *Fall*.

Drop-down skeg A type of fin that can be raised and lowered by the paddler.

Dry top/dry cag A type of garment for the upper body that keeps the paddler dry and prevents water entering the top of the sprayskirt. Also called a 'dry paddling jacket'.

Eddy A phenomenon that occurs where a river current is obstructed, causing it to swirl back upstream behind the obstruction.

Eddy-hop To move from one eddy to another on a rapid.

Eddy line/fence/wall The interface between current and eddy.

End grabs Handles at each end of the boat for carrying, towing or general hanging on.

Ender Term used to describe a boat standing on end in the water.

Entrapment Getting trapped or held against a solid object by the force of the water.

Fall Any significant slope or step down in a current, but usually means waterfall. See *Drop*.

Feather The angle between the paddle blades or the act of turning them. Also called 'twist'.

Feature Generic term kayakers apply to any hydrological phenomenon on a river.

Feedback Kinaesthetic awareness of forces acting upon you, the boat or the paddle.

Ferry glide A way of crossing a current without being swept downstream. Sometimes just called 'ferrying'.

Flailathon My name for any loss of control that results in ineffective gymnastics or paddle-waving.

Flare A rocket that fires a bright light into the air to attract attention at sea.

Following Wind or waves coming from behind. See *Tailwind*.

Foredeck The deck of the boat in front of the cockpit.

Forward Towards the bow/front of the boat.

Future water The bit of water a kayaker intends to move into next.

Grade/grading A system for describing the severity or difficulty of a rapid, from 1 to 6 (or I to VI). Synonymous with class.

Green water Nothing to do with its colour really – means water that isn't white/bubbly/aerated. Sometimes called 'hard'.

Grip The way you hold the paddle.

Ground swell Confusing term for the pattern of deep-water waves that will be surf when they reach land.

Gunwale The side or top edge of the boat.

H or HI rescue Emptying a kayak between two others while afloat.

Hand roll Self-righting the kayak without getting out, using only bare hands.

Haystacks Unstable, exploding waves.

Headwind A wind that's blowing in your face.

Helix A freestyle trick – an aerial 360° spin, for at least 180° of which the boat must be inverted.

High brace A way of keeping your balance by resting weight on the front (drive-face) of the paddle blade.

Hip flick/rotation/snap A balancing/rolling skill – rotates the boat along its long axis.

Hull The underside of the boat.

Inuit Native inhabitants of the Arctic from whom the word kayak is derived.

Isometric tension Muscles applying force without the body part actually moving.

J stroke A stroke canoeists use to keep the boat going straight while only paddling on one side. Mysterious to kayakers.

Karabiner A type of climbing hook/shackle that's used for all kinds of things in the world of kayaking.

Kayak A boat paddled with one or more two-blade paddles while sitting facing forwards.

Kayaker A person who paddles a kayak. See also *Boater*.

Leash Device for attaching kayaker to boat or paddle, or boat to paddle.

Leeward The downwind direction or side.

Lid Widely accepted colloquial term for 'helmet'.

Loom The shaft of the paddle.

Loop Freestyle trick – a somersault, effectively. Term previously referred to any instance of standing the boat on end in the water.

Low brace A way of keeping your balance by resting weight on the back of the paddle blade.

Meltdown A way of descending a drop or fall by passing underneath the hydraulic below it. Opposite of boof.

Micro eddy A very small eddy with room for only one kayak.

Moment of inertia Maths term – defines how hard something is to turn. Nothing to do with time. See *Swing weight*.

Open water A big, wide expanse of water, typically a sea or lake, but can be a huge, flat river.

Overfall A type of rapid formed by seawater, caused by waves or tide spilling over rocks.

Overthruster A plastic pod that supports the sprayskirt and increases the volume of the boat.

Paddler Generic term for a canoeist or kayaker. See *Boater*.

Park and huck Driving to a waterfall to descend it, without paddling down the whole rapid or river.

Park and play Driving to a wave to play/freestyle on it, without paddling the whole rapid or river.

Peeling wave When the top of a wave curls over and begins to break along its face.

PFD Personal flotation device or buoyancy aid.

Phoenix Monkey Freestyle sequence – a 360° pirouette followed by a loop.

Pin/pinned Getting trapped or held against a solid object by the force of the water.

Pin spot A place where there's a significant danger of physical entrapment.

Pitch Tipping the boat forwards or backwards.

Planing Travelling fast enough that the hull generates lift.

Playboat Specialised type of kayak with very low, flat ends that can slice easily into the water to facilitate tricks and three-dimensional paddling.

Pocket/power pocket/zone The critical position in the shoulder of a surf wave.

Pop Describes the way the kayak can 'pop' up out of the water after being partially or completely submerged. Used a lot by whitewater paddlers. More pop = more height. Also, to 'pop' the deck or skirt of a kayak means to remove it.

Portage The act of carrying the kayak around an obstacle or undesirable section of water and putting it back into the water on the other side.

Pourover A nasty type of river feature made by water flowing over all sides of a boulder.

Purling Describes when the bow of the boat catches or buries in the water.

Rapid A turbulent section of fast-flowing water.

Ratchet strap A type of webbing strap with a mechanical tensioning buckle for tying kayaks to vehicles.

Recirculate To be repeatedly carried back upstream by an eddy or hydraulic, unable to escape it.

Rib Ridge or groove designed to stiffen a paddle or kayak.

Rocker The amount that a boat's hull is turned up at the ends.

Rocket cross Technique for crossing a current by getting the kayak to plane.

Rocket move Technique for projecting the kayak a long way by leaping off the top of a wave.

Roll Tipping/rotating the boat to the left or right.

Rudder A type of skeg that's controlled by the kayak to aid steering.

S-cross Crossing a river by breaking into the current on one side, heading briefly downstream, and breaking out on the other.

Sculling Imparting a force by slicing the paddle quickly from side to side in the water.

Seal launch Launching the boat by getting in it on land and then sliding into the water. Unclear if that's because the boat is 'sealed' already or it's because that's what seals do!

Seam Where two currents converge and turn downwards; the join between deck and hull of a kayak.

Seaward The side nearest the sea, furthest from shore.

Shaft The cylindrical part of the paddle that you hold. Also called the loom.

Shockcord A type of elastic rope that's used a lot in marine environments. Also called bungee.

Shoulder The edge of the breaking section of a wave.

Shuttle The vehicle used for, or the act of, transporting kayakers or gear by road to the opposite end of a paddling trip.

Siphon Anywhere that the current flows under or through an obstruction like a tree or pile of rocks, with no air space.

Skeg A type of fin to help the kayak track (go straight) well.

Ski A sit-on-top type of kayak.

Slack water Water that isn't moving on a river, or around the time of high or low tide on the sea.

Splitwheel A cartwheel with a 180° edge transition between the two phases.

Spraydeck/sprayskirt Equipment for sealing the cockpit of a kayak to keep water out.

Squirt boat A type of super-low-volume whitewater kayak designed for sub/trans-surface use.

Stern The back part of the boat.

Stick Widely accepted colloquial term for 'paddle'.

Stirring My word for practising paddle feedback, by moving the paddle around in the water.

Stopper A recirculating breaking wave on a rapid, so named because it can stop and hold a kayak or swimmer.

Strainer An obstruction through which the current flows, acting like a sieve to trap kayaks or swimmers.

Support stroke Any stroke that rights the boat or prevents it from tipping over more.

Swift water Alternative name for white water.

Swim/swimming Kayaker jargon for ending up in the water minus kayak.

Swing weight How difficult something is to turn/rotate. Sometimes known as 'moment of inertia' or 'rotational mass'.

Swirlathon When the current or wave overpowers you and tosses you around like flotsam.

Swirly The kind of twisty-turny water that provokes a swirlathon.

Symmetrical A paddle with the top and bottom edges of its blade the same length.

Tailwind A wind at your back.

Throwline A type of rescue rope used by kayakers.

Tippy A word lots of people told me I couldn't use in a book. Wobbly, or unstable.

Touring Travelling the waterways by kayak.

Towline A proprietary tow rope used by kayakers.

Track/tracking The ability of a kayak or kayaker to hold a straight line.

Transit Making a straight-line open water crossing from one specific point to another.

Tricky Woo Freestyle sequence – splitwheel with 180° pirouette on the tail using only one stroke.

Trimming Adjusting the boat in pitch or roll.

Tuiliq Inuit kayaking jacket.

Upwave Towards the top or crest of a wave; seaward side of a wave.

Upwind Towards the source of the wind, wind in your face.

Volume (kayak) Refers to how much air/buoyancy is contained in a kayak, measured in litres/gallons.

Volume (river) Refers to how much water is flowing down a river, measured in cumecs (cubic metres per second) or cfs (cubic feet per second).

Water blade The blade of the paddle that's in the water during a stroke.

Weathercocking When a kayak constantly veers towards the wind or swell.

Weir An artificial barrier across a river that the water pours over like a waterfall. Unlike a natural waterfall. Because the water flow can be so even and the bottom made from concrete and/or metal superstructure, these are often incredibly dangerous.

Whirly/whirlpool A type of vertical vortex in a rapid, like the water spiralling down a sink or drain.

White water Water that's bubbly/aerated by turbulence. Rapids.

Windage The degree to which something is affected by the wind.

Windward The side the wind is coming from.

X rescue Emptying a kayak across the foredeck of your own boat while afloat.

Yaw Change of direction left or right.

ACHNOWLEDGEMENTS AND PICTURE CREDITS

A book like this relies heavily on its contributors and sponsors, without whom I would have been scratching around taking photos of old kayaks in friends' garages, and frankly it wouldn't have looked half as good! I would like to mention my sincere thanks to all of the photographers, whose names appear opposite and are annotated with the locations of their contributions. I'd also like to thank Pete Astles, James Bebbington, Ron Fischer, Chris Hobson, Freya Hoffmeister, Eric Jackson, Howard Jeffs, Thomas Mazimann, Rafael Ortiz, Alex Rodegro, Ben White and Helen Wilson for their help and anecdotes, autobiographies and photos. Furthermore I must thank the fantastic people at the following companies who supplied time and kayaking product: Big Dog White Water Kayaks, Kober Paddles, Nookie The Paddling Company, North Shore Kayaks, and Valley Sea and Surf Kayaks.

Nikki Ball, Ruth Beavis, Alexandra Crichton, Joanne Davies, Spencer Doane, Joshua Gosling, Phil Hurley, Aled Price, Coral Mcaulay, Dan Thomas, Peter Thompson, Richard Ticehurst and Hazel Wilson donated their time, paddling skills and infinite patience to helping me shoot the technique stuff. Jade Aldridge, Gemma Kitty James, Chanelle Jobe, Darrell Lindsay, Russell Main and Leanne Ward gave up their time to help with on land shots. A number of other unnamed paddlers also feature in the photos, and I hope they too like what they see. Epic Kayaks, Folbot Folding Kayaks and Lettmann GmbH supplied invaluable photos, Madison UK provided GoPro waterproof cameras and Lowepro the camera bags that organise, protect and transport it all. I extend my gratitude to all of the above, and anyone I may have forgotten, and hope that they like the book that their efforts made possible.

PICTURE CREDITS

Pete Astles – 154, 157tr, 158, 159 all
Michelle Basso – 105bl
Felicity Bell – 60 main, 64t, 65t
Mariano Buenoventura – 134
Raimund Bulczak – 74
Steve Childs – 9 all, 31mr, 89t, 91t, 116
Pete Copp – 90t
Steve Cosner – 80 header
Andy Coulter – 112, 113
Austen Davies – 14t, 91b, 92
Folbot Folding Kayaks – 7, 15m, 72, 76bl, 80br
Joshua Gosling – 8tr, 29mr, 101, 135tr, 136, 170/171
Richard Hobson – 165 main
Lane Jacobs/Red Bull Content Pool – 96 main
Katya Kulkova – 109tr, 111 main & inset, 161b
Anja Lettmann 138
Marsport – 157b, 162, 163 all.
Alfredo Martinez/Red Bull Content Pool – 96 inset
Pierre Mellows – 32br, 152t, 153t, 153m
Ville Miettinen – 8br
Nookie The Paddling Co. – 78b, 84
Alexandre Schaal 160 tr
Lars Schneider – 14l, 77 all
Frank Schröer – 106t
Helen Stewart – 33m, 94t, 95bl, 149
Seppi Strohmeier – 104
Bjorn Thomassen – 1, 6, 47tr, 88, 94b, 95tr, 172/173
Mark Tozer/Helen Wilson – 86 all
Lucas Tozzi/Epic Kayaks – 93 main
Isabella Tulloch – 58bl, 59br, 83
Balint Vekassy – 164 all
James Weir – 81, 82b
Kevin Wilcox – 80t
All other photos © **Bill Mattos**

USEFUL ADDRESSES

BRITISH CANOE UNION HQ
(also the offices of Canoe England)
18 Market Place, Bingham, Nottingham NG13 8AP
Tel: 0845 370 9500 or 0300 0119 500 Fax: 0845 370 9501
www.bcu.org.uk

SCOTTISH CANOE ASSOCIATION
Caledonia House, South Gyle, Edinburgh EH12 9DQ
Tel: 0131 317 7314 Fax: 0131 317 7319
www.canoescotland.org

WELSH CANOEING ASSOCIATION
Canolfan Tryweryn, Frongoch, Bala, Gwynedd LL23 7NU
Tel: 01678 521199 Fax: 01678 521158
www.canoewales.com

CANOE ASSOCIATION OF NORTHERN IRELAND
Unit 2 Rivers Edge, 13-15 Ravenhill Road, Belfast BT6 8DN
Tel: 02890 738 884
www.cani.org.uk

USA CANOE/KAYAK NATIONAL OFFICE
(Oklahoma City, OK)
Attn: Joe Jacobi
725 South Lincoln Blvd. Oklahoma City, OK 73129
Tel: 405 552 4040 ext. 4504
www.usack.org

CANOEKAYAK CANADA
2197 Riverside Drive, Suite 700, Ottawa, Ontario K1H 7X3
Tel: 613 260 1818 Fax: 613 260 5137
www.canoekayak.ca

AUSTRALIAN CANOEING
PO Box 6805, Silverwater, NSW, 2128 Australia
Tel: 02 8116 9727 Fax: 02 8732 1610
www.canoe.org.au

NEW ZEALAND
www.rivers.org.nz – Whitewater NZ
www.canoeracing.org.nz – Canoe Racing NZ (Kayak)
www.canoepolonz.org.nz – Canoe (Kayak) Polo NZ

WATER SAFETY AND RESCUE TRAINING
www.rescue3.com – The standard in water and
rope safety education